# UDL NOW!

## A Teacher's Guide to Applying Universal Design for Learning in Today's Classrooms

Katie Novak

ISBN 978-1-9305836-6-5
E-book ISBN: 978-1-9305836-7-2

Published by:
CAST Professional Publishing
an imprint of CAST, Inc.

40 Harvard Mills Square, Suite 3, Wakefield, MA 01880
www.castpublishing.org
publishing@cast.org
Tel: (781) 245-2212
TDD/TTY: (781) 245-9320

Cover and Interior Design by:
Happenstance Type-O-Rama

# Contents

# Foreword

By David H. Rose

This revised and expanded edition of *UDL Now!* is a timely and welcome addition to the growing literature about Universal Design for Learning. The first edition was a huge success. Katie Novak's well-articulated know-how about how to put UDL into practice has helped many thousands of educators. However, rather than rest on that success, Katie has done what expert learners and expert teachers do: she has reflected on her own performance and asked, "What can I do better? How can I make my point clearer? What have I learned from those many practitioners I have met and worked with in the past couple of years?" Throughout this book, you'll find the answers to those and other questions. The result is a bigger and better book.

One of the most basic aspects of UDL is representing key information in more than one modality: images are described, spoken language is captioned, texts are spoken aloud. Providing those multiple representations is key to ensuring that information is equally accessible for all learners. With new technologies, these multiple representations of images, texts, and sounds are easy to create.

Unless the original is art.

Making art accessible is very different, and much harder, than making information accessible. Artists stretch the boundaries of their medium, using paint or instruments or words in novel ways that evoke rich and complex emotions like awe, inspiration, solemnity, sublimity. To render art accessible requires capturing that "stretch" of the medium, the originality and the emotions that follow. That is much harder than capturing information.

Consider, for example, one of Monet's paintings of waterlilies at Giverny. It is easy to describe the "information" in the painting: "A small pond with a bridge in the background and waterlilies on the surface of the pond." Obviously that description, while accurate, fails to capture the *art* of Monet at all. Indeed, no amount of verbal description will capture what makes Monet's painting great, what makes it beautiful, sublime. To capture Monet's art in words will require something more like poetry than prose.

Great teaching looks a lot like art. While there has been a great deal of attention lately to the "science" of teaching, it is the art of teaching that we most remember and that strikes us with awe. And that is hard to describe or codify.

Katie Novak is an artist when she teaches. I have seen her. She does things that awe and inspire; watching her is like watching a master sculptor at work. Everyone should have a chance to see her teach—and especially to see her bring UDL to life.

But most of you won't see her in action, so how can the art of her teaching be captured and described? Fortunately, Katie is also an artist with words. She can describe what she does, as only an artist can, without evaporating the awe, the joy, the sublimity, of what great teaching is really like.

Welcome to her art. Welcome to it now.

# Preface to the Revised Edition

The reality show, *Survivor*, has been a hit in the United States since its debut in 2000. The premise of the show—arrive in an isolated location, form alliances, engage in challenges, don't die—has been the topic of countless conversations throughout its thirty plus seasons. While other reality shows have come and gone (i.e, *Dating in the Dark*, *Are you Smarter Than a 5th Grader?*), *Survivor* has flourished by providing viewers with locales from Borneo to Nicaragua, organizing strategic, creative challenges, and creating tribe configurations that foster collaboration and community with competitors we can't help but root for. From the Survivor All-Stars to Brain vs. Beauty, the winners have one thing in common: they are motivated, resourceful and strategic about their game. In UDL, we call them expert learners, but they are more than that. They are models of persistence and grit, and how the human spirit, when ignited and engaged in rigorous challenge, can succeed, despite obstacles.

In 2014, *UDL Now: A Teacher's Monday Morning Playbook for Implementing the Common Core Standards Using Universal Design for Learning* was published. Think of it at season one. When I penned that first edition, I wrote about what I knew then. Now, three years later, I have a much better understanding of the journey of all educators, PK-12, the barriers they face, and the tools they need to be successful. The overall premise of this book is the same – arrive in a learning environment, form professional learning communities, engage in universally designed instruction, and don't give up – but this is like an all-star edition because it has been informed and inspired by countless educators across the country who have invited me into their practice and shared their experiences and the work of their students. By stepping outside my classroom, I have learned that expert teachers, just like our favorite Survivors, are models of persistence and grit, and succeed, despite obstacles, when ignited and engaged by the UDL framework.

# Introduction

Just for a second, imagine education reform as one giant dating pool. You, the teacher or administrator, are an eligible education bachelor or bachelorette and you're just waiting for some education initiative to sweep you off your feet, change your practice, and turn you into John Keating, the inspiring high school English teacher played by Robin Williams in *Dead Poets Society*.

If you've been teaching for a while, you've probably flirted with many promising and very suitable education initiatives, but I imagine, like me, you've broken it off with them, saying, "It's not you. It's me." Case in point: I actually made a T-shirt for my district's "Looking at Student Work" enterprise—a bright yellow V-neck

**Objective:** *After reading this introduction, you will understand the appeal of Universal Design for Learning (UDL) and why its implementation is vital for all teachers and learners.*

**Rationale:** UDL is best practice. The research in this text has been outlined in Appendix A. Rather than rehash that here, this introduction presents an analogy that will make the concept of UDL more concrete and introduce you to the shift the UDL framework requires.

with ironed-on decals that read, "Got student work?" I practically skipped into the library for our first meeting, clutching a portfolio of student work for "warm" and "cool" feedback. It didn't last long. You know where that shirt is now? Dusting my end tables.

Naturally, I was skeptical when administrators at my school tried to set me up with UDL. I would teach as I always had and hope for the best. But they persisted and convinced me to attend a weeklong UDL workshop at CAST. Once I learned what UDL was all about, I couldn't resist. Too good to be true? Absolutely not. It's the real thing, "a keeper," as my mom would say. If UDL had to write a personal ad, this would be it:

> About me and who I'm looking for: I never met a brain I didn't like. Seriously, every teacher and every learner is intriguing and capable, and I promise that if you contact me, I will appreciate and value you for everything you are. (Read: I will not try to label you or fix you.) My interests are your interests. Love sitting down quietly to read? I'll be there with novels, newspapers, and poems, with titles that are engaging to you. I can bring you the hardcover classics with the cracked spines, or I can download the text to your e-reader. If it's been a long day and your eyes are tired, I'll read to you in a smooth, confident voice. Are you more of a visual person? Let me show you the world through movies, pictures, paintings, and colors. We can communicate through art, comics, and sketches. Are you more of a mover? Let's dance, rap, put on skits, and discover things on our own. I'm also excellent with technology, though there's so much more to me than that. If you don't have any technology at all, we can still have a great relationship. I will never put you in a new or uncomfortable situation without preparing you for it. I'll listen to your concerns, minimize any threats, and practice with you until you feel comfortable. You will always feel valued, always feel understood, and always feel capable. Call anytime—or stop by in person, e-mail, text, glog, make a Snapchat, tweet, post a Facebook update, send a carrier pigeon . . . whatever helps you communicate best.

If you're a UDL veteran, you're probably nodding your head right now. Like any good relationship, you've made it work by putting in a lot of time and commitment.

If you're new to UDL, you may have one of the following scenarios playing in your head, all of which make you want to close this book and donate it to the library. Let's address these right away so you aren't tempted to quit too soon.

**Scenario 1** You love the idea of UDL but don't think you have time to create the lessons. Believe me, you're not alone. Every teacher has some combination of the following: new curriculum or state standards, new textbook, new standardized test, a new state evaluation tool, parent meetings, department meetings, IEPs, 504s, RTI, multi-tier systems, and SSTs.

**Scenario 2** You feel like UDL is being forced on you. For example, maybe your new evaluation tool is aligned with the principles of UDL so you're reading this book because you have to. You may be feeling frustrated because someone is telling you how to teach. Well, you're not alone. Professionals hate being told what to do. Doctors probably hate washing their hands hundreds of times a day while staring at reminders to wash their hands, but they do it. Why? Because no one wants to be the patient of the surgeon who says, "I don't like being told what to do," and wipes her hands on her pants.

**Scenario 3** You have learned about UDL, and it all sounds a little too much like UDLtopia. You believe in the framework, but maybe it doesn't seem realistic. This could be for a variety of reasons. Some practitioners believe that UDL would work extremely well with older students, but that elementary students aren't yet capable of becoming expert learners. Others feel as though UDL would work for motivated learners, but student behaviors would prevent a teacher from delivering a curriculum with so much embedded choice.

If any of these scenarios represent how you're feeling right this minute, you need to know that UDL is a curriculum-design process that saves you time over the long haul *and* frees you to make your teaching practice more effective, while honoring your individual approach. UDL will ignite your passion for your craft, while also helping to increase student learning at all levels. I have seen UDL work in classrooms preK–12, using the strategies outlined in this text. I have seen teachers transform students of all variability into expert learners by teaching them how to learn. Many students do not arrive at school with a toolbox full of executive function and self-regulation skills, but UDL provides teachers with the set of strategies to embed the development of these skills within a rigorous curriculum. UDL is where the science and the art of teaching are blended, and although you may feel like you're about to climb a mountain, know that the view from the top will be worth it.

If you ask anyone who has been married for 50 years, he or she will tell you that a strong marriage is not built overnight. The same is true for UDL. I recently heard someone say that it takes 100 tries to become proficient at a task. I am sure that 100 is an arbitrary number, but the message is clear. If you want to develop a skill, you have to provide countless opportunities to practice that skill. We can consider this "100 tries" as it relates to us as educators, and to our students.

When you start implementing UDL, you may be starting at number 1, the proverbial first try. Just know that the longer you stick with it, the closer you are to reaching 100, or becoming a UDL expert. Have faith that the commitment is worth it, and someday soon, you will look back fondly at your first try and appreciate your journey. The same is true for our students. It may take 100 tries for our students to become self-directed, motivated, knowledgeable, resourceful learners, but we owe it to them to facilitate that journey. You may work hard all year and take students from 1 to 30, and it may feel like you failed, but you did not. You have made things that much easier for the next teacher, and the one after that. Eventually, there will be a teacher who gets to see the 100th try—the moment when learning clicks—and maybe that teacher will get all the credit. But that student will always know that you were an integral part of that success.

This book aims to take you on a journey so you can design standards-based lessons that engage students in the learning process. The following chapters include hundreds of content-specific and content-neutral lesson ideas that you can use as-is or easily adapt for your own classroom use, regardless of what grade you teach. If you like what you see, just make a copy. Want to change something? Use the online component to make it perfect for you. All templates in this text are available at www.katienovakudl.com/udlnow. In closing, it's important to note that this book focuses on implementation from a practical perspective. If you want to see the research on UDL's effectiveness, please read any of the titles in Appendix A, "UDL Resources."

# 1

# UDL and Reality TV Collide

Implementing UDL is a little like being a contestant on *The Biggest Loser*. Don't laugh. Individuals apply to be on *The Biggest Loser* because they feel stuck in a rut and want more out of life. These people often are hard-working, smart individuals who have lots of diet advice at their fingertips yet are still not able to lose weight. It's not for a lack of trying, but rather they seem to lack the tools and support necessary to be successful. Education is kind of like that. New initiatives come and go like fad diets. Like yo-yo dieting, it's easy to get off track and go back to our old habits when we don't have the necessary support.

This happens on *The Biggest Loser*. When participants have Jillian Michaels whipping them into shape

**Objective:** *You will understand the importance of having the support of administrators and colleagues when you shift from traditional teaching strategies to UDL.*

**Rationale:** Because UDL requires a change of practice, you'll have more success if you have the support of administrators and colleagues. One great way to do this is to create or join a professional learning community (PLC). This text has an embedded PLC guide to help you accomplish that task. This chapter will explain the importance of having support while transitioning to UDL and how to use the PLC resources, if you're interested.

and their peers cheering them on, it's easier to be successful. Unfortunately, when some of these people return home, they put the weight back on. It's not that they don't know how to exercise and eat, because they do; it's a lack of support pushing them to reach their goals. People who want to accomplish the same goal need each other.

As teachers and administrators, we need to lean on each other. We need to celebrate our successes and push each other to the next level of our practice. Can we be successful on our own? Of course we can. But it's much easier when we have colleagues to support us, teach us, and cheer us on—and who depend on us to do the same for them. Especially now.

American education is changing, so we have to change, as well. New evaluation tools, new curriculum standards, and new standardized assessments are big initiatives that require change. The persistent gap between our highest and lowest students requires change. We need our students to be college ready or prepared for their chosen career. They deserve to be successful. Their success is, in part, up to us. What an amazing privilege. Our teaching strategies can change students' lives, so we owe it to our kids to give them the very best. UDL is the very best.

The nation depends on us to mold the future of America. Granted, students have a part in it, too, but research suggests that we teachers provide three of the four key ingredients in the learning mix (Fenstermacher & Richardson, 2005). The four ingredients necessary for students to learn are:

- The learner's own effort
- The social surround (family, community, and peers)
- The opportunity to learn
- Good teaching

Although teaching appears to account for only one of the four variables, an effective teacher has the potential to influence student effort and the opportunity to learn. Student effort is considered, in part, a teacher's responsibility, because a teacher has an opportunity to set up a classroom that engages students and makes them more likely to persist, despite obstacles. Teachers can also influence a student's opportunity to learn by providing the kind of structure that allows students to spend an appropriate amount of time on-task.

As you probably noted, although effective teaching has the potential to influence three of the four learning variables, teachers cannot influence the social surround of family, community, and peer culture. The communities and homes where some students live often create significant obstacles to learning, but there is evidence that some classrooms can raise student achievement, despite these problems. How extraordinary is that? As teachers, we can literally overcome the negative influence of a community. How many other professionals can say that? That's practically a superpower.

We all have to believe at our core that we can engage and challenge all students to learn in our classrooms. We can't prevent all the challenges students will face, but we can help to alleviate them by designing a learning environment that leaves no room for failure. To do this, we need to be surrounded by people who have that same belief in the power of teaching. This increases our own efficacy, that is, our ability to teach all students.

Teachers with strong feelings of efficacy believe they will be successful, and they have better outcomes than those who believe that they will not succeed. These teachers are committed to student learning, but also to each other. They work toward common goals. They prod and help each other, and their students, to achieve those goals. This group mentality is called collective efficacy (Goddard, Hoy, & Hoy, 2000) and relates to Dweck's (2006) work on the importance of growth mindset.

We are all likely familiar with the classic children's tale, *The Little Engine That Could*. Her mantra, which has become a cliché in the world of perseverance, "I think I can, I think I can," is a valuable message that we, as educators, need to embrace.

Growth mindset is based on the simple premise that we are much more likely to succeed if we believe that effort, and not inherent skill, intelligence, and talent, will result in success. The opposite of growth mindset, fixed mindset, is the belief that some things in life are simply out of reach. In classrooms, we hear students say, "I can't do that." Teachers will sometimes admit to me, "I'm just not really effective with *those* kids." *Those* kids: the classification or grouping is irrelevant.

All teachers and students need to believe inherently that they are capable of improving their performance by applying necessary effort, seeking out information and resources, collaborating with others who are more knowledgeable, and repeating throughout the process, "I think I can."

In comes *The Biggest Loser*. The participants on the show are so successful because while they live on *The Biggest Loser* campus, professionals teach and model the basics of healthy living. The guidelines of the show are simple: eat less and exercise more, practice moderation in all things, and lean on the group for support. Participants are able to change their bodies and their lives because their lifestyles are aligned to scientifically based research, and they are given a solid support system. *The Biggest Loser* emphasizes the importance of collective efficacy, which is why contestants cook, eat, exercise, and live together. When they feel like they can't go on, they have a group of like-minded individuals to remind them that they can change if they have a growth mindset. In order for UDL to be a success and have staying power in your teaching practice, you need the same.

Now, on the reality show, participants are thrown together for a couple of months. As a teacher, you have your colleagues for your career. There is no reason to fall back on old habits when you have a built-in support system in your building. Administrators, that includes you, too!

First, you need to learn about the scientifically based research, which you can access in other UDL texts (see Appendix A) and on the National UDL Center's website, www.udlcenter.org.

Second, you need the tools to put the research into practice. This text provides you with concrete examples of UDL implementation, as do others in a growing body of literature supporting UDL practice (see Appendix A). *Universal Design for Learning in the Classroom: Practical Applications* (Hall, Meyer, & Rose, 2012) and *Universal Design for Learning: Theory and Practice* (Meyer, Rose, & Gordon, 2014) are two examples.

Finally, you need a support system. Just as new teachers need to adjust to the profession, new UDL teachers need to adjust to the pedagogical shifts UDL requires. When you begin UDL implementation, you need to move away from "fixing kids" to "fixing curriculum," and this takes time and creativity. Having a support system will make this transition much easier.

Figure 1-1 outlines the phases new teachers go through in their first year (Moir, 1990). These may be the same phases you go through when you adopt UDL as a framework in your learning environment. In this model, teachers move through six phases. Let's examine how these phases may be similar for teachers implementing UDL and why support can minimize the feelings of disillusionment mid-year. In the anticipation phase, you learn about the UDL framework and you're excited to implement it in your classroom. Maybe you've attended a UDL workshop or read a book, or maybe your district has adopted UDL district-wide. Let's face it, you probably have images of engaged students applauding you at the end of a life-changing lesson (hey, we can dream, right?).

**Phases of First-Year Teacher's Attitude Toward Teaching**

**FIGURE 1-1:** Phases of First-Year Teaching (adapted from Moir, 1990)

The issue is that once you start to plan UDL lessons, you realize that it takes a lot of thought, creativity, and time. You realize that it was easier to just lecture or have students read silently. At this point, you may be getting frustrated because UDL lessons take so much time to plan. It's important at this stage to realize that you don't need to change everything at once. Although you have the option to hit UDL full throttle, you can also begin by making incremental changes in your learning environment, such as implementing aspects of UDL that you can draw on daily as you progress. You may plan only one UDL lesson a week at first. Then, as you become more comfortable, make additional changes to your practice. Just implementing some of the guidelines of UDL each day will make a difference in student engagement and achievement. At this point, it's most important to remember not to panic. It may seem like a lot of work, but it will get easier with time, and student learning will increase.

If you're feeling overwhelmed by the shift to UDL, it's great to have a support group with colleagues. Once you start implementing UDL into your classroom, you begin to speak a whole different language, and if no one else speaks your language, you'll feel a bit isolated. I don't know if any of you have ever tried a Rosetta Stone language-learning program, but my mother-in-law did, and she's not speaking French. She was trying to learn the language by herself, and there was no one to talk to. When you're learning a new language, you need to speak to people who speak that language.

Realizing that changing your practice is a process will help you to avoid the disillusionment phase, where you may feel like you were better off before you tried to change everything. Your colleagues here are so important, because the more you can share your struggles, the more you'll realize it's just a phase and that students are benefiting from the changes you're making.

Think of this period like *The Biggest Loser* weigh-in (I know, I just won't let it go). The weigh-ins are all about collective efficacy. Participants don't want to let their teammates down. They're in it together. By the same token, as you share with your colleagues, you will want to share stories about the frustrations and celebrations of becoming a UDL pro, and this will make you accountable. Also, there will be people there to celebrate your small successes.

You will begin to see results, and this, in turn, will rejuvenate your practice. When *The Biggest Loser* participants see the weight start to melt off, they work out harder and eat healthier. In the first couple of episodes, everyone is miserable, but in the end, they are all healthier and happier because they learned that the practice works. You will feel the same. You may set out to implement UDL lessons once a week, but once you see how engaged your students are, you'll want to do more and more. And believe me, if you keep at it, you will see gains in student achievement. The scale never lies.

At the end of each school year, remember to reflect on your practice and think about the wonderful changes you've made. You can then begin to anticipate next school year and how you can use more UDL strategies more often.

Because UDL support is imperative for effective practice, it is beneficial when teams of teachers adopt UDL as a framework and work together to implement strategies. If UDL is being encouraged at the district level, you will probably have more supports in place. If it's something that you are implementing on your own, start recruiting ("Come on, everybody is doing it").

UDL implementation will not happen overnight. Think of it as a lifestyle change as opposed to a diet. The UDL Implementation Process (Figure 1-2) is a five-step, multiyear process that begins with a need for change.

As a nation, we are not meeting the needs of all students by providing them with access to a rigorous, engaging curriculum. By reading this book, you are exploring and preparing to implement UDL. Although it looks like a climb to expert learning, know many teachers have gone before you and enjoyed the view from the top. And hiking with a group is a heck of a lot easier than tackling the mountain alone.

To support you even more on your climb, know that your accountability group is about to increase exponentially. In December 2015, a new federal education law, dubbed the Every Student Succeeds Act (ESSA), endorsed UDL as best practice, so all of the nation's 3.5 million teachers will need support as they design and deliver comprehensive instruction that "incorporates the principles of universal design for learning."

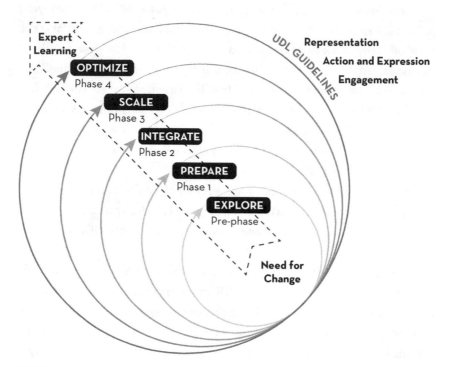

**FIGURE 1-2:** UDL Implementation Process. © CAST, 2014. Used with permission.

One great way to get fellow teachers interested in UDL is to form a professional learning community (PLC), which is like a study group. Often, teachers join book clubs to read *New York Times* bestsellers, but they are hesitant to join a PLC because it feels like work. It shouldn't be work. It should be something that will ignite passion about your profession. If it does feel like work, at least it's work you would be doing anyway. It's like a double dip of your time. These are lessons you would've planned, but you'll get priceless suggestions from colleagues, and professional development credit. Most importantly, you will understand how to create dynamic, challenging lessons that will engage all students. Better yet, when you try out the lessons on students, you'll have a group of people to brag to about how awesome you are and how well your students performed!

In order to help you make the most out of your PLC, this text includes an embedded discussion guide and action steps so you can begin to implement UDL in your practice in a meaningful way. In a recent article, "The Futility of PLC Lite," the authors note that PLCs often fail to change teacher practice or increase student achievement because they do not focus on curriculum design or evidence-based decision making (DuFour & Reeves, 2016).

DuFour and Reeves (2016) note that in meaningful PLCs, teachers grapple with four core questions:

BINGO

- What do we want students to learn?

- How will we know if they have learned it?

- What will we do if they have not learned it?

- How will we provide extended learning opportunities for students who have mastered the content?

Learning about and implementing UDL allows teachers to focus on these core questions as a tenet of their practice. UDL is a standards-based framework that guides teachers to heighten the salience of goals and objectives in order to design engaging, challenging learning experiences that allow all students to become knowledgeable, strategic, and motivated. Also, in an effective PLC, teachers collectively set appropriate goals for learning and design and administer assessments without barriers so they will know when students have mastered the content or skills. Lastly, effective PLCs consider the importance of varying demands and resources to optimize challenges for those students who have not learned the content or skills, or who need additional challenges. If your PLC doesn't consider these questions, it will "fail to embrace the central tenets of the PLC process and won't lead to higher levels of learning for students or adults" (DuFour & Reeves, 2016).

To help you facilitate a PLC in your school or on Twitter, this text has an embedded discussion guide to use with your colleagues that will lead you to reflect on the important questions that are necessary to improve outcomes for your students. If you are an administrator, encourage groups of teachers to form PLCs, or you can do the activities with your entire staff. The discussion questions and practice prompts are great activities if you're working alone, but you can get even more out of them if you have others to bounce ideas off of. If there is no one in your school who wants to join your PLC, you can hook up with other like-minded teachers on Twitter by searching for #udlchat.

In addition to discussion questions at the end of each chapter, there are also four opportunities for practice, or assessments you'll create for students, throughout the text. The assessments will serve two purposes. One, many districts require teachers to turn in evidence to support their participation in a PLC. Two, and most importantly, you can use the assessments with your students immediately. This text will have all the resources you need to actually plan student lessons, and once you make them, you'll begin to internalize the process, and you can use it every day. The four practice points are easy to identify because they are preceded with stars, like this one:

A full description of the PLC, and a pacing guide, is in Appendix B, "Professional Learning Community Resources." You can submit the guide and your completed work to your district office to get professional development credit if you choose to complete the PLC in house.

## SUMMARY

A shift in teaching practice is similar to a new weight loss program—both endeavors require a growth mindset, commitment, time, and support. Support is important because it will increase collective efficacy and make it more likely that all teachers will continue to implement UDL, even when moving through phases similar to those new teachers go through. I encourage teachers to form or participate in PLCs in their own schools to enlist other teachers to implement UDL simultaneously.

# DISCUSSION QUESTIONS

1.  Think of all the teaching initiatives you have been encouraged to try in your career. Which ones do you continue to implement and which ones were phased out? Why do you think some strategies remained in your practice while others did not?

2.  Why is collaboration so important when changing teaching practice? When losing weight?

3.  Think about times in your life when you experienced the power of collective efficacy. What was the experience like for you?

4.  How does the concept of collective teacher efficacy affect student learning?

# 2

# The UDL Guidelines for Educators

*A Planning Tool You Can't Live Without*

Before we delve into curriculum design and delivery, you must be familiar with the Educator Guidelines, which are a list of teaching tips created by CAST, the UDL gurus. These tips will help you to design UDL lessons.

To understand the Guidelines, it is important to start with the big picture. In its most basic definition, UDL is thoroughly knowing the concept you're going to teach and presenting that concept in different ways while engaging the students and encouraging them to express their knowledge in different ways.

Some teachers examine the Guidelines, choose one or two that fit into their current practice, and say, "I teach UDL" or "I do UDL." Although it's great that many educators implement

**Objective:** *You will understand the building blocks of UDL—the Guidelines—and be able to paraphrase them.*

**Rationale:** In order to implement UDL in classroom instruction, you must be familiar with the Guidelines. This chapter "unpacks" them, clarifying difficult concepts. Since the Guidelines are the building blocks of a universally designed curriculum, developing a deeper understanding of them and mastering their content will help you in the lesson-planning process later.

some guidelines of UDL already, it's a mistake to think that using one or two guidelines equates to full implementation. UDL isn't something you can just "do." UDL is what your practice becomes when you shift the way you think about teaching and learning.

Simply put, UDL is not a checklist. A UDL teacher doesn't just play a video and hand out a rubric. He or she eliminates barriers to learning by proactively and deliberately planning curriculum that all students can access. The key word is *proactively*. UDL guides conscious, planned decisions to help all students learn the standards you are required to teach.

This may be a big philosophical shift for some, because historically it was a teacher's job to "fix" the students so they could succeed in a standardized way. Although this was well intentioned, times have changed. Our job now is to teach all students to meet high standards by providing flexible and varied avenues to success—using the means *the students* most need, as individuals, to succeed. We have such limited time with students. Instead of wasting time trying to transform them from individuals into standardized learners, we need to teach them as they are and allow them to be the most successful people they can be. It's profound, really, to think about teaching that way, and also very liberating. We are now free to embrace our subject matter, to think creatively, and to help students love the content as much as we do.

As stated in the previous chapter, we cannot fix students' home lives, and we cannot fix the communities where they live, but we also can't make excuses. Instead, we have to set the bar high and develop a curriculum that will inspire and challenge all students. To do this, we need to focus on how our students will be successful. If you think about all the reasons why your students will not be successful, they won't be. This is called the *deficit model*, and unfortunately many schools and teachers operate in this mind-set.

The deficit model blames student failure on the students, their parents, and the community (Prime & Miranda, 2006). Teachers who function under this model believe that their students do not have what it takes to succeed, and no amount of teaching will change that. Because of their low sense of efficacy, teachers lower their expectations. They change the sequence and pace of instruction and deemphasize challenging topics, simplifying others. This is *not* UDL. UDL is all about designing lessons that will challenge all students and push them to achieve grade-level standards. When you teach

UDL, you have to believe that all your students will succeed and keep that belief at the forefront when designing your curriculum. If you eliminate barriers in your learning environment, you take away many of the reasons and excuses for failure. Then, and only then, you can teach every student.

Note that this is not creating a challenging curriculum and then modifying it later. That is reactive and aligns more closely to the differentiated instruction (DI) framework, which will be discussed in more detail in Chapter 3. UDL is about taking your skill, your passion, and your craft and designing your lessons with embedded options so they are relevant, accessible, and challenging to all students.

To look at this another way, imagine you are having a dinner party for some new colleagues. You'll probably plan a menu that plays to your strengths as a cook or utilizes the best catering in your area so you can stay in your comfort zone as a host. This is very similar to the traditional style of teaching, because teachers teach in their comfort zones; administrators facilitate meetings in their comfort zones.

Now, imagine that all day, to get ready for your party, you've worked hard to prepare Mexican lasagna. If you've never made it, it's basically traditional lasagna with the following substitutions:

| TRADITIONAL ITALIAN LASAGNA | MEXICAN LASAGNA |
|---|---|
| Instead of lasagna noodles... | Flour tortillas |
| Instead of ground beef with marinara sauce... | Ground turkey seasoned with taco seasoning, a jar of salsa, a can of black beans, and a can of corn |
| Instead of a blend of mozzarella, ricotta, and parmesan cheese... | Sharp cheddar and spinach leaves |

You're feeling optimistic and totally prepared because the lasagna looks and smells delicious and the house is clean. You light some candles, hear a knock at the door, and welcome your guests. Everything goes great, until dinner. As you serve the meal, you realize that not everyone can eat it.

- Pat is on the Paleo Diet, so he can't have dairy.

- Kristen is a vegetarian, so she can't eat the ground turkey.

- Jessie is on a gluten-free diet, so she can't eat the tortillas.

What are you, a good host, to do? You rush around making accommodations so your guests can eat. You have some leftover ground turkey, so you make Pat a turkey burger and throw a handful of raw spinach leaves on his plate. Kristen can eat a cup of beans and corn. Jessie can just pick around the tortillas, right? The problem is all your guests are not getting the same wholesome, balanced meal.

Compare this to teaching. When we teach the way we always have, some of our "guests" cannot consume what we're serving and have to eat scraps. If they can't eat, they become starved, and then we turn around and call them picky eaters.

Now, if you were a UDL menu-planner, you would have thought more about the possible barriers of your guests and planned one delicious meal they would've enjoyed together, or you would've provided more of a "make-your-own" Mexican night with different options, including the ingredients for salads, tacos, and burritos with ground turkey, tofu, and sautéed vegetables. If you had planned the meal proactively from the beginning, you would have eliminated the barriers and would not have had to make unnecessary accommodations.

If you were planning a UDL menu, you would not reduce the meal to its lowest common denominator. For example, braised tofu on a bed of lettuce would allow everyone to eat, but would leave some of your guests hungry. The magic of hosting is to provide enough options that everyone can fill their plates (and their bellies) with food that is delicious and nourishing, and that meets their dietary needs. You don't want your guests swinging through the drive-through on the way home.

Once you plan your menu of options, you also have to consider the tools that you will provide so your guests can serve themselves. While collaborating with a group of teachers, a high school history teacher noted that there's much more to planning a buffet than considering the options for the meal. An effective, proactive party planner also considers the importance of providing utensils, plates, bowls, and napkins. You could plan a delicious Mexican taco buffet but if you don't provide your guests with serving spoons, plates, and utensils, the dining experience won't be fully accessible for your guests. In short, everyone is likely to make a mess.

Let's take the dinner party "tools" analogy and relate it to teaching. Think about a common barrier that prevents students from completing their work: the lack of a writing utensil. In a perfect classroom, every student would come prepared to class, but for many of us, this is not the norm.

Imagine you've designed a writing lesson where students are required to read a local newspaper, either in hard copy or online, and then respond to the editor. Their response should influence the attitudes or actions of a specific audience on an issue.

One student, Tim, comes to class without a pencil (for the 50th time this year). You have a couple of options. Choose the most UDL-friendly option. (Hint: It's the one that eliminates the barrier and allows Tim to show his understanding of the task.)

**A.** Send Tim to the office to sit for the period. His lack of preparedness is a problem and he needs a consequence.

**B.** Allow Tim to sit in class without a pencil. Have him finish the writing assignment for homework.

**C.** Have a student resource center where Tim can borrow a pencil without interrupting the class, or allow him to use his device to type or audio-record his response.

**D.** Stop the class and ask if anyone can lend him a pencil. Wait while students rummage through their backpacks to find one.

**E.** Give Tim a pencil but deduct 10% off his grade on the assignment.

If you chose C, you're thinking like a UDL teacher. Not having a pencil is an obstacle or a barrier for some students. Remember that ultimately, your job is to support Tim as he attempts to influence his audience as he responds to text. He can only meet the standard if he can participate with you and his classmates and he has the correct tools.

Option A does not align with the UDL approach because if Tim isn't in the classroom, he can't engage in the lesson and learn how to write the response. As a result, Tim cannot meet the standard.

Option B is not correct because Tim deserves to get immediate mastery-oriented feedback on his writing, and he will not have access to you or his peers if he is unable to work toward the standard.

Option D is not correct. Although you are giving Tim a pencil, you have taken class time away from learning. As a teacher, you have a great number of standards and very little time to cover them.

Option E is not correct because Tim's grade should reflect his progress toward meeting the learning standard, not meeting classroom rules.

Another example of a barrier to learning is student behavior. I once observed a star teacher, Patty, who was channeling UDL principles in her classroom management plan. Patty worked in a low-performing urban school, but her students were nearly perfectly behaved for the entire 90-minute period. At the end of the class, she explained that it was because they knew they would never get away with it because they knew that "she would handle it." Patty said that she would never expel a student from the room for being disruptive. For many students in urban schools, she explained, that is what they want. She went on, "I never send kids out . . . never. I tell them I make a commitment to educate them for 90 minutes a day, and I can't educate them if they are out of the room."

Her policy? When a student is disruptive, she or he must have a lunch date with Patty. When a student has a lunch date, Patty takes out a box of fine linens and flickering battery-powered candles and sets a table for two. During lunch, Patty sits with the student and tries to understand why she or he was acting out in class. She has been having lunch dates since she began teaching. She joked, "No kids ever have lunch dates more than once." She went on to explain the responsibility she felt for her students: "I must educate these kids between 8 and 3 because they're not going home and getting any education. If I don't do it, they won't get it at all." If behavior is a barrier, remove the barrier, not the student.

UDL is not just about providing tools for students to access learning experiences and managing your classroom. It's about eliminating barriers so every student can succeed. One way to start is to use the UDL Guidelines. If you've already been introduced to UDL, you've probably seen the Guidelines, version 2.0, published by CAST in 2011, which numbered the principles, guidelines, and checkpoints (Figure 2-1). All the guidelines and checkpoints are invaluable resources for teachers, but for some educators the numbered format seemed to suggest a hierarchy, where Representation was more important or prominent than Expression and Engagement.

# Universal Design for Learning Guidelines

| I. Provide Multiple Means of **Representation** | II. Provide Multiple Means of **Action and Expression** | III. Provide Multiple Means of **Engagement** |
| --- | --- | --- |
| 1: Provide options for perception<br>1.1 Offer ways of customizing the display of information<br>1.2 Offer alternatives for auditory information<br>1.3 Offer alternatives for visual information | 4: Provide options for physical action<br>4.1 Vary the methods for response and navigation<br>4.2 Optimize access to tools and assistive technologies | 7: Provide options for recruiting interest<br>7.1 Optimize individual choice and autonomy<br>7.2 Optimize relevance, value, and authenticity<br>7.3 Minimize threats and distractions |
| 2: Provide options for language, mathematical expression, and symbols<br>2.1 Clarify vocabulary and symbols<br>2.2 Clarify syntax and structure<br>2.3 Support decoding of text, mathematical notation, and symbols<br>2.4 Promote understanding across languages<br>2.5 Illustrate through multiple media | 5: Provide options for expression and communication<br>5.1 Use multiple media for communication<br>5.2 Use multiple tools for construction and composition<br>5.3 Build fluencies with graduated levels of support for practice and performance | 8: Provide options for sustaining effort and persistence<br>8.1 Heighten salience of goals and objectives<br>8.2 Vary demands and resources to optimize challenge<br>8.3 Foster collaboration and community<br>8.4 Increase mastery-oriented feedback |
| 3: Provide options for comprehension<br>3.1 Activate or supply background knowledge<br>3.2 Highlight patterns, critical features, big ideas, and relationships<br>3.3 Guide information processing, visualization, and manipulation<br>3.4 Maximize transfer and generalization | 6: Provide options for executive functions<br>6.1 Guide appropriate goal-setting<br>6.2 Support planning and strategy development<br>6.3 Facilitate managing information and resources<br>6.4 Enhance capacity for monitoring progress | 9: Provide options for self-regulation<br>9.1 Promote expectations and beliefs that optimize motivation<br>9.2 Facilitate personal coping skills and strategies<br>9.3 Develop self-assessment and reflection |
| **Resourceful, knowledgeable learners** | **Strategic, goal-directed learners** | **Purposeful, motivated learners** |

**FIGURE 2-1:** Universal Design for Learning Guidelines 2.0 (2011)

To remove this misconception, or barrier, CAST has issued a new representation of the Guidelines that is reformatted (Figure 2-2) to put Engagement first and strip away the numbers. The Guidelines themselves are still the same, but the new format will make it easier for some users to grasp the idea that all three principles are equally important to attend to. Think of the revision as UDL for UDL.

The Engagement, Representation, and Strategy Guidelines correlate to the way our brains are organized for learning. UDL is built on years of research in the learning sciences, including brain science, focused on three networks of the brain. Think of the networks as the three areas of the brain that help students learn. If you can tap into all three networks in a lesson, your students will learn more.

Students will learn more because activating all three brain networks does what it says: it ensures that three parts of the brain are turned on and ready to learn. To give you an image, think back to the commercial produced by the Partnership for a Drug-Free America in the 1980s—the one that played relentlessly during after-school specials. The commercial zoomed into a cast-iron skillet, with butter sizzling in a pan. The voiceover said, "This is drugs." Then, an egg is cracked, drops to the pan, and begins to char in the scalded butter. The same voice says, "This is your brain on drugs." Preteens everywhere were traumatized by that commercial, imagining their own brains spilling out of their ears like burnt yolk. The message was clear: drugs can ruin your brain, and then you can't learn. That's because the drugs burn networks or areas of the brain to make certain tasks difficult to impossible.

If we were to develop a UDL commercial today, we could take a page from the book of the anti-drug initiative, except in reverse. Instead of butter, the first image could be violet, raspberry, and cobalt-blue Easter egg dye in porcelain bowls. Then, they could cut to an egg so beautifully dyed that it appears like a Fabergé egg sitting in all its glory on a gold pedestal. "This is your brain on UDL," James Earl Jones would croon (his voice never gets old, does it?).

If you can light up different parts of the brain, students will learn. If you fail to light up those brain networks, you're in fried-egg territory, and it will be difficult for students to learn anything from you.

# Universal Design for Learning Guidelines

| Provide Multiple Means of **Engagement** *Purposeful, motivated learners* | Provide Multiple Means of **Representation** *Resourceful, knowledgeable learners* | Provide Multiple Means of **Action and Expression** *Strategic, goal-directed learners* |
|---|---|---|
| **Provide options for self-regulation** <br> +Promote expectations and beliefs that optimize motivation <br> +Facilitate personal coping skills and strategies <br> +Develop self-assessment and reflection | **Provide options for comprehension** <br> +Activate or supply background knowledge <br> +Highlight patterns, critical features, big ideas, and relationships <br> +Guide information processing, visualization, and manipulation <br> +Maximize transfer and generalization | **Provide options for executive functions** <br> +Guide appropriate goal-setting <br> +Support planning and strategy development <br> +Enhance capacity for monitoring progress |
| **Provide options for sustaining effort and persistence** <br> +Heighten salience of goals and objectives <br> +Vary demands and resources to optimize challenge <br> +Foster collaboration and community <br> +Increase mastery-oriented feedback | **Provide options for language, mathematical expression, and symbols** <br> +Clarify vocabulary and symbols <br> +Clarify syntax and structure <br> +Support decoding of text, mathematical notation, and symbols <br> +Promote understanding across languages <br> +Illustrate through multiple media | **Provide options for expression and communication** <br> +Use multiple media for communication <br> +Use multiple tools for construction and composition <br> +Build fluencies with graduated levels of support for practice and performance |
| **Provide options for recruiting interest** <br> +Optimize individual choice and autonomy <br> +Optimize relevance, value, and authenticity <br> +Minimize threats and distractions | **Provide options for perception** <br> +Offer ways of customizing the display of information <br> +Offer alternatives for auditory information <br> +Offer alternatives for visual information | **Provide options for physical action** <br> +Vary the methods for response and navigation <br> +Optimize access to tools and assistive technologies |

**FIGURE 2-2:** Universal Design for Learning Guidelines (2013)

The three brain networks match up with the UDL Guidelines. The Guidelines provide tips about how to activate each network. Sometimes you'll hear people refer to the "networks" and others refer to the "Guidelines," but they are more or less referring to the same thing.

The Guidelines are the building blocks of a UDL curriculum, and because I'll refer to them throughout the book, it's important that we review them now so we have a common understanding going forward. If you're already familiar with the Guidelines and the networks and feel you don't need a refresher, skip ahead. As you saw in the Guidelines (Figure 2-2), there are three columns. The first column includes the Engagement Guidelines. There are two significant barriers to engagement (Table 2-1). The first is that students don't think the curriculum is interesting or relevant to them so they don't care to learn. The second is that students lack perseverance or coping skills and they cannot persist when learning gets challenging. If either of these barriers is present in your learning environment, it doesn't matter how brilliantly you design your curriculum. Students have to believe that learning your content or skills matters or they can choose *not* to learn.

**TABLE 2-1:** Barriers to Engagement

| AFFECTIVE OBSTACLES |
| --- |
| Students don't understand the purpose of the lesson. |
| Assignment is too easy or too difficult. |
| Assignment has no value in students' lives. |
| Student's lack of coping strategies or other self-regulation functions. |
| Subject matter is deemed boring or irrelevant. |
| Students are embarrassed. |

The Engagement Guidelines are so valuable, because making curriculum relevant, and instilling grit in students, cannot be delivered by a scripted curriculum and pacing guides. You are a teacher and you know your students. Connecting your curriculum to your audience and giving them the tools to stay motivated is a true art. Providing multiple means of engagement will help you to do this more effectively and activate students' affective networks.

You don't necessarily have to implement every Guideline with every student. The Guidelines remind you to provide options. If, for example, you aim to "Prevent students from getting upset or quitting by giving them scaffolds, positive reinforcement, break time, and so on," you may have a subset of students who do not want to take a break from their learning. That's okay. In UDL, students are empowered to direct their own learning. With all Guidelines, you will focus on providing the options and helping students to reflect on the options and choose the most appropriate ones.

Implementing the Engagement Guidelines will help you to eliminate some common barriers that prevent students from becoming motivated, purposeful learners (see Table 2-2).

**TABLE 2-2:** Engagement Clarified

| PROVIDE MULTIPLE MEANS OF ENGAGEMENT | TRANSLATIONS |
|---|---|
| Provide options for self-regulation.<br><br>• Promote expectations and beliefs that optimize motivation.<br><br>• Facilitate personal coping skills and strategies.<br><br>• Develop self-assessment and reflection. | • Offer students tips on how to stay motivated and provide resources to prevent frustration; allow students to work in groups, use mentors or coaches, or just provide tips on how to persist and work with a text.<br><br>• Prevent students from getting upset or quitting by giving them scaffolds, positive reinforcement, break time, and so on.<br><br>• Encourage students to assess their own learning by using checklists and rubrics. |
| Provide options for sustaining effort and persistence.<br><br>• Heighten salience of goals and objectives.<br><br>• Vary demands and resources to optimize challenge.<br><br>• Foster collaboration and communication.<br><br>• Increase mastery-oriented feedback. | • Ask students to restate a lesson's standard or objective and remind them about it often throughout the lesson.<br><br>• Provide varying levels of challenge so students can pick assignments that are not boring or too difficult for them.<br><br>• Allow students to work together.<br><br>• Give feedback often throughout each lesson using various methods like self-reflection, peer review, and teacher feedback. Don't just give feedback on final assessments. |

**TABLE 2-2:** Engagement Clarified  *CONTINUED*

| PROVIDE MULTIPLE MEANS OF ENGAGEMENT | TRANSLATIONS |
|---|---|
| Provide options for recruiting interest.<br><br>• Optimize individual choice and autonomy.<br><br>• Optimize relevance, value, and authenticity.<br><br>• Minimize threats and distractions. | • Allow students to make choices so they are more likely to be engaged in the curriculum (more on this in Chapter 7).<br><br>• Tell students at the beginning of a lesson why it will be relevant to them. Make the connection explicit.<br><br>• Create a classroom environment where students feel safe and can express knowledge in ways that are best and most engaging to them (more on this in Chapter 4). |

The Representation Guidelines remind us to provide multiple means of representation to activate all students' recognition networks. *Representation* is the process of teaching new content or skills to students. Historically, reading and lecturing were popular teaching methods, so let's examine some of the barriers associated with them (Table 2-3).

If we teach in only one way and don't provide students with options, some students won't learn. Since it's our job to teach all students, we must use multiple representations for every lesson we teach. The Guidelines provide reminders, or suggestions, on how to do this. Every time you plan a unit, have the Guidelines in front of you to ensure you're aligning your curriculum to them.

**TABLE 2-3:** Presentational Barriers

| BARRIERS IN THE LECTURE FORMAT | BARRIERS IN READING TEXT |
|---|---|
| Hearing impairment. | Poor vision. |
| Attention issues. | Inability to decode the text. |
| Poor memory. | Poor reading comprehension skills. |
| Lack of background knowledge. | They read slowly and they don't have enough time to get all the information. |
| They don't understand the vocabulary or subject-matter jargon you use. | They don't understand the vocabulary (either because it's too difficult or because they don't know how to read). |
| Your language is not their first language. | |

There are 12 checkpoints, or specific teaching strategies, to examine when designing the Representation portion of your lesson (Table 2-4). The table has two columns. The left column has the Guidelines as they are written. In the right column, vocabulary is clarified in language that may be more accessible.

**TABLE 2-4:** Representation Clarified

| PROVIDE MULTIPLE MEANS OF REPRESENTATION | TRANSLATIONS |
|---|---|
| Provide options for perception.<br><br>• Offer ways of customizing the display of information.<br><br>• Offer alternatives for auditory information.<br><br>• Offer alternatives for visual information. | • Provide digital copies of all class materials so students can access and personalize them (great if your students have 1:1 devices).<br><br>• Don't just lecture to students. Provide visuals and hard copies so all students can access at least one of the mediums.<br><br>• Don't just have students read. Also provide audio, visuals, and things for them to manipulate if they choose. |
| Provide options for language, mathematical expressions, and symbols.<br><br>• Clarify vocabulary and symbols.<br><br>• Clarify syntax and structure.<br><br>• Support decoding of text, mathematical notation, and symbols.<br><br>• Promote understanding across languages.<br><br>• Illustrate through multiple media. | • Preteach vocabulary and math symbols in student-friendly language.<br><br>• Point out text structures (like compare/contrast), sentence structure, or math formulas if they are important for learning.<br><br>• If you provide reading, provide scaffolding to bring student attention to most important content.<br><br>• If English is a second language for students, offer instructions in their home language(s) or provide visuals to support comprehension.<br><br>• Simplify complicated directions to make student friendly and/or use visuals to increase understanding.<br><br>• Always offer visuals like charts, pictures, movies, audio clips, and things for students to touch and manipulate. |

**TABLE 2-4:** Representation Clarified *CONTINUED*

| PROVIDE MULTIPLE MEANS OF REPRESENTATION | TRANSLATIONS |
|---|---|
| Provide options for comprehension.<br><br>• Activate or supply background knowledge.<br><br>• Highlight patterns, critical features, big ideas, and relationships.<br><br>• Guide information processing, visualization, and manipulation.<br><br>• Maximize generalization and transfer. | • Remind students what they already know about the content. If nothing, teach the necessary information.<br><br>• Make it clear what the most important information is by modeling comprehension strategies such as monitoring, highlighting, asking questions, and note taking.<br><br>• Provide work exemplars, explicit directions, and scaffolds so students can persist through the lesson.<br><br>• Help students see how they can use the new information in other classes, units, or settings. |

The Action and Expression Guidelines focus on strategies to access and support student learning. It's imperative to engage students and represent content so it's accessible, but in order to determine if students have learned content, you must assess their learning. Two popular methods to assess students are written responses and objective paper/pencil tests. Let's look at some barriers of these formats (Table 2-5).

**TABLE 2-5:** Barriers to Action and Expression

| BARRIERS TO WRITTEN RESPONSES | BARRIERS TO OBJECTIVE TESTS |
|---|---|
| Lack of a writing utensil or electronic device to keyboard response. | Test anxiety. |
| Poor handwriting or keyboarding skills. | Lack of a writing utensil. |
| Poor motor skills. | Questions are skipped/answers are tracked incorrectly. |
| They don't know proper format. | Misunderstood or misread directions. |
| Poor at spelling and/or grammar. | Lack of strong test-taking techniques. |
| Don't communicate well in writing. | Poor recall/memory. |

Provide as many options as you can for students to express their knowledge and to activate their strategic networks. If that is not possible, then prompts need to include built-in scaffolds, work exemplars, and explicit directions for all students. There are nine checkpoints, or teaching strategies, to examine in the Action and Expression Guidelines (Table 2-6).

**TABLE 2-6:** Action and Expression Clarified

| PROVIDE MULTIPLE MEANS OF ACTION AND EXPRESSION | TRANSLATIONS |
|---|---|
| Provide options for physical action.<br><br>• Vary the methods for response and navigation.<br><br>• Optimize access to tools and assistive technologies. | • Give students the option of composing with different media (writing, typing, physically manipulating objects, and so on) when completing assignments.<br><br>• Allow students to use technology to express knowledge like using speech recognition software, typing, and so on. |
| Provide options for expression and communication.<br><br>• Use multiple media for communication.<br><br>• Use multiple tools for construction and composition.<br><br>• Build fluencies with graduated levels of support for practice and performance. | • Give students choices about how they will respond (see Chapter 7 for lesson examples). Instead of just writing a response, they could perform a skit, make a poster, create a Microsoft PowerPoint presentation, and so on.<br><br>• Allow students to complete assignments using different tools. Some students may complete assignments on paper, others may use a 1:1 device, while others may record audio. Provide students with the multiple tools to complete assignment: dictionaries, thesauruses, IPads, voice recognition software, calculators, handouts with necessary formulas, and exemplars.<br><br>• Build scaffolding into every assignment and provide feedback while students are working (see Chapter 8). |

**TABLE 2-6:** Action and Expression Clarified *CONTINUED*

| PROVIDE MULTIPLE MEANS OF ACTION AND EXPRESSION | TRANSLATIONS |
|---|---|
| Provide options for executive functions.<br><br>• Guide appropriate goal-setting.<br><br>• Support planning and strategy development.<br><br>• Facilitate managing information and resources.<br><br>• Enhance capacity for monitoring progress. | • Begin all assignments with an objective and rationale and provide work exemplars, scaffolds, and checklists for every assignment.<br><br>• At the beginning of each assignment, give student tips and checklists to help them work through the assignment or ask them to create their own strategy for completing the task.<br><br>• Give students a lot of tips on how to stay organized while they are completing each assignment and make necessary resources like highlighters, graphic organizers, and calculators accessible. Some students don't know how to organize things on their own.<br><br>• Have students reflect on their learning by asking questions, and always provide many opportunities for students to get feedback before completing final drafts. |

If you want your students to become knowledgeable, goal-directed, motivated learners, plan your lessons using the Guidelines. In each lesson you design, use as many of the checkpoints as you can. The more checkpoints you use, the more likely you will be able to influence student effort and students' opportunity to learn, which are two key ingredients in the learning mix.

Now, after learning about the UDL Guidelines, you're probably feeling one of three ways:

**A.** Excited

**B.** Overwhelmed

**C.** Skeptical

Remember, whatever you're feeling is normal, but let's try to shed a little light on those three emotions, because many other teachers have felt the same way.

If you're excited, that's wonderful. This is probably because you've heard of UDL before, and you're interested in implementing it in your practice. UDL is a great way to get students motivated and increase achievement. Maybe you've already started implementing UDL, and now you're psyched because you are feeling affirmed and ready to do more. Good for you!

If you're feeling overwhelmed, that's okay too. UDL is a lot of work, but just take a step back and realize that you don't have to implement everything at once. You can't go from 0 to 60 in a blink. Remember that it may take 100 (or more) tries until you've hit your stride. Try to design one complete UDL lesson each week if that is possible and then make an effort to make small adaptations in your learning environment, like posting a standard on the board or allowing students to choose how they will respond to new content. You don't have to completely change overnight. You can begin to implement UDL right away, but you won't be hitting every checkpoint in every lesson from the start. It's like training for a marathon. When you're first training for such an event, it seems like you'll never get there when you're running only a mile, but those miles start adding up, and the same will happen with your UDL practice.

Maybe you feel skeptical whenever you hear about new education reform because it's so frustrating that best practices seem to change yearly. You probably hate wasting time planning units that are thrown away the next year. The thing is, UDL has already been around for over 25 years, and it's not going anywhere. My best advice is to just try it. If you fully commit to teaching one UDL lesson, you'll see a change in your students and that's not something you'll ever feel skeptical about.

## SUMMARY

The UDL Guidelines provide a practical, scientifically based method that will improve your daily teaching and curriculum design. Keep them posted on your desk as a great reminder of how you want to teach every day.

# DISCUSSION QUESTIONS

1.  Which UDL Guidelines/checkpoints do you use already with students? It may be helpful to go back and highlight all the strategies you use on a regular basis.

2.  Which UDL Guidelines/checkpoints would you have a difficult time implementing? Ask yourself why. Do you think students would not be receptive to them, or do you think you would have a difficult time with the strategy? Why? If you're with colleagues, ask them their opinion.

3.  How do you feel about the fact that student effort is theoretically under a teacher's control? Does it feel like too much responsibility? Why or why not?

4.  Think about the best lesson you have ever taught. How did you know it was such a success? Which Guidelines/checkpoints were at work in that lesson?

5.  Think of one lesson you have taught recently that was a bomb. Looking at the Guidelines/checkpoints, were there any barriers in that lesson that could have been avoided by using some of the suggestions?

# 3

# Shining a Light on Engagement

Consider for a moment, two very different types of leaders. One leader, Ms. Micromanager, controls every aspect of your practice. Without even asking for your feedback, she dictates your professional goals, how your classroom is set up, and the protocols for your parent meetings. You don't find that level of support useful (that's putting it nicely), but you comply because, after all, she's your boss. Another leader, Mr. Autonomous, hires you because he believes you are capable of great things. He supports you with the resources and feedback you need to be successful, and he provides you with options for how to organize your classroom and structure parent meetings. Which boss are you willing to work harder for?

**Objective:** *You will understand how UDL's focus on student engagement and empowerment is what distinguishes the framework from differentiated instruction (DI).*

**Rationale:** Many educators view the UDL Guidelines and wonder, "Isn't this the same thing as DI?" The answer is no. Both approaches address traditional education's failure to meet the needs of all learners. But UDL focuses much more on designing for all rather than individual students. And it focuses more on student engagement and empowerment. This chapter will focus on the importance of focusing on engagement when delivering universally designed education.

In his 2009 book *Drive: The Surprising Truth about What Motivates Us*, Daniel H. Pink discusses this crucial difference between compliance and engagement. He notes that, "control leads to compliance; autonomy leads to engagement" (p. 108). Engagement leads to motivation or "the desire to get better and better at something that matters."

So, let's step back and think about the weight of that. If we want our students to be motivated learners, we have to support their journey so they become autonomous and can personalize their learning. To do this, we have to focus on engagement and start with *why?* Empowering our students with options and the opportunity to personalize their own learning is one of the core concepts of UDL and what sets it apart from differentiated instruction (DI). Some teachers may see the Guidelines and say, "Isn't this just DI with a different name?" The answer is no. Although the two frameworks share similarities, there are significant differences. To be clear, both DI and UDL are ways to differentiate curriculum to meet the needs of students. DI, however, is more reactive and teacher directed (the learning options are often controlled by the teacher) whereas UDL is proactive and student directed (which allows students to become autonomous learners). Table 3-1 provides a visual representation of the spectrum from traditional education to DI to UDL.

**TABLE 3-1:** Traditional, DI, UDL Education Scale (Adapted from Bartholomew Consolidated School Corporation [2012])

| TRADITIONAL EDUCATION | DIFFERENTIATED INSTRUCTION | UDL |
|---|---|---|
| Static | Reactive | Proactive |
| Evaluates the curriculum | Evaluates the student | Evaluates classroom environment and culture |
| Follows scripted lesson | Adapts script when it's not effective | Intentional |
| Teaches curriculum as design | Retrofits instruction by providing accommodations | Designs instruction prior to students arrival with embedded choices |

**TABLE 3-1:** Traditional, DI, UDL Education Scale (Adapted from Bartholomew Consolidated School Corporation [2012]) *CONTINUED*

| TRADITIONAL EDUCATION | DIFFERENTIATED INSTRUCTION | UDL |
|---|---|---|
| Designed for the average students | Designed for different groups of students based perceived ability | Designed for students of all variability |
| Does not consider students in the margins | Plans different learning experiences for students in the margins | Plans for all students |
| Ignores barriers | Works around barriers | Eliminates barriers |

Traditional education was static and was focused on following a script. Teachers were subject matter experts, not learning experts, and the rigor of the content reigned supreme. For a long time, traditional education worked because students in the margins were educated in separate settings. If you reflect back to Psychology 101 in college, you may remember the bell curve (Figure 3-1).

| LOW | AVERAGE | HIGH |
| PERFORMERS | PERFORMERS | PERFORMERS |

**FIGURE 3-1:** The Bell Curve

Before inclusion, the students in the margins (i.e. "low performers" and "high performers") were often not educated with their peers. Because there was less variability in the classroom, teachers could deliver a lesson as it was designed and most students would "get it." Granted, they may have been bored out of their minds, but they were compliant, so traditional education prevailed.

Finally, after years of separate education for students in the margins, the nation embraced the concept of inclusion, which was a huge step in the right direction. With all learners in the classroom, teachers soon realized that the traditional education was not accessible to some students. As a result, DI was born. Teachers reacted to the needs of students and created differentiated learning experiences for students who struggled or who needed enrichment.

In this model, teachers looked toward individual students and provided entry points, learning tasks, and outcomes that allowed those students to access the curriculum (Hall, Strangman, & Meyer, 2003). In this model, teachers created different levels of expectations for students so they could be successful (Waldron & McLeskey, 2001). The limitation of this model is that all students do not have access to the same rigorous education. Choices are made for students and controlled by the teacher, without providing students with the opportunity to set their own goals, create their own strategies, and choose the learning experiences that best meet their needs. In short, DI provides multiple means of representation and expression, but does not provide for multiple means of engagement at the same level as UDL. UDL has an increased focus on building students' executive function and self-regulation, and engaging them throughout the learning process, while continuing to provide multiple means of representation and expression so they can become autonomous learners.

Many educators who hear about UDL for the first time are already familiar with DI. If that's you, don't feel like you have to start over. If you're already familiar with DI, you're in a great place because you're already teaching in an inclusive environment, and you're thinking about how to provide multiple levels of challenge to your students. You're on the road to UDL and all the work you've done to learn about DI is important groundwork for this next step. Now it's time to start with the *why* and empower our students to think critically about how to make choices about their own learning.

*Why* is at the core of the human experience. Simon Sinek (2011), an expert on motivational leadership, designed a graphic called the Golden Circle (Figure 3-2), which puts *why* at the center. Sinek explains, "Put simply, it helps us understand why we do what we do. The Golden Circle provides compelling evidence of how much more we can achieve if we remind ourselves to start everything we do by first asking why" (p. 38).

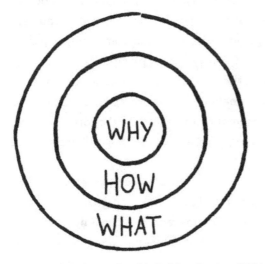

**FIGURE 3-2:** Simon Sinek's Golden Circle © 2016, Simon Sinek. Used with permission.

Our students need to know *why* they are learning and *why* it's important to persist when learning gets hard. And this is equally important whether learners are in pre-K or experienced teachers attending professional development. Let's examine the importance of *why* in a first-grade class, and then in a PD session, so it's clear that all learners are more engaged when teachers provide multiple means of engagement.

Imagine a first-grade teacher sitting in a rocking chair at circle time. The teacher opens the book *Kindness Is Cooler, Mrs. Ruler,* and starts with *why.* "Today, we are going to read a book about being kind. This is really important because as a school we have been preparing for World Kindness Day. This book may be challenging, but since you are all super-readers and have a growth mindset, you will be able to read all about how Mrs. Ruler's class learns to be kind. You will have a couple of choices for reading. You can read it by yourself or with a small group, you can read it while listening to it on the headphones, or you can sit with me and I will read it with you. It doesn't matter what anyone else picks. You choose what is best for you, and don't worry—you can change your mind. For example, if you try to read by yourself, remember our tricks about 'just-right books.' Can anyone tell me how you can tell if a book is just right? That's right. If there are three words on a page that you can't read, you may want to change your strategy. Can someone remind me what a strategy is?"

While focusing on the *why*, the teacher builds engagement by giving students choices, minimizing threats and distractions, encouraging students to set their own goals, promoting expectations that optimize motivation, facilitating personal coping skills, and developing self-assessment. In UDL, start with the *why*.

Note in this example how the students are empowered through engagement. The teacher did not assign students to groups based on reading levels; she encouraged autonomy, and she challenged them to define their own goals and coping strategies when reading, all while creating a motivating, warm environment.

Starting with the *why* is not just effective for our PK–12 students. It's the best thing for all learners, including you. Right now, I'm going to take you through a short reflection. I want you to close your eyes (metaphorically . . . keep reading) and reflect on one or more terrible professional development experiences you've had during your career. Now, I want you to build an imaginary box called Bad PD. Take those memories one by one and place them in the box. You know the ones: the seminar where the presenter read PowerPoint slides until you were dizzy, the time the presenter was a complete know-it-all, and the keynote presenter who threw mini candy bars into the audience promising a big "Pay Day" if you adopt the newest teaching strategy. (True story. Hit someone right in the face.) When you peer into this Bad PD box, you will not see a lot of sessions that adhere to the UDL Guidelines about providing multiple means of engagement. Instead, you'll likely see all the opposite, the Anti-Guidelines if you will (see Table 3-2).

**TABLE 3-2:** The Anti-Guidelines for Engagement

| PROVIDE MULTIPLE MEANS OF ENGAGEMENT | BAD PD: THE ANTI-GUIDELINES |
|---|---|
| Provide options for self-regulation<br><br>• Promote expectations and beliefs that optimize motivation<br><br>• Facilitate personal coping skills and strategies<br><br>• Develop self-assessment and reflection | Does not provide options for self-regulation<br><br>• Boils teaching and learning down to standardized test scores—not a big catalyst for teacher motivation<br><br>• Doesn't provide you with optional resources that you can use to clarify concepts, such as sticky notes and markers<br><br>• Only asks for feedback during the last 30 seconds when you're filling out the evaluation |
| Provide options for sustaining effort and persistence<br><br>• Heighten salience of goals and objectives<br><br>• Vary demands and resources to optimize challenge<br><br>• Foster collaboration and communication<br><br>• Increase mastery-oriented feedback | Does not provide options for sustaining effort and persistence<br><br>• Multiple times during the presentation you lean over to a colleague and say, "Why are we here?"<br><br>• There is only one presentation with few options to review background information or explore application in relevant ways.<br><br>• No group work. Just practice your listening skills.<br><br>• Presenter doesn't provide you with feedback on how the PD relates to your practice. |
| Provide options for recruiting interest<br><br>• Optimize individual choice and autonomy<br><br>• Optimize relevance, value, and authenticity<br><br>• Minimize threats and distractions | Does not provide options for recruiting interest<br><br>• You are required to attend. Period. End of story.<br><br>• The presenter's examples don't relate to your grade or subject area.<br><br>• The presenter yells, seems angry, or gets defensive when you question the relevance of the proposed PD. |

When considering the importance of engagement, first-grade students aren't so different from us, as adult learners. We also need to start with the *why* of learning so we can make our own decisions and become autonomous learners.

Let's return to our two leaders from the beginning of the chapter—Ms. Micromanager and Mr. Autonomous—and put them in front of the classroom. Ms. Micromanager makes decisions for her students based on their abilities. Even if her decision is appropriate, a critical aspect of UDL is missing. Students never had the opportunity to set goals for their learning and they weren't given the opportunity to hone their executive function and self-regulation strategies. These are important if we want all our students to be successful in whatever paths they choose.

Mr. Autonomous planned similarly for his lesson. He created opportunities for students that reflected various levels of challenge and provided students with supports and scaffolds such as work exemplars, rubrics, and graphic organizers. The key difference is that Mr. Autonomous provided students with control of their own learning as he supported them with mastery-oriented feedback. Not only are students learning important content, but they are learning how to be learners, which is a lesson that they will carry with them forever. I will leave you with this question: Who are the students willing to work harder for?

## SUMMARY

When delivering UDL lessons in the classroom, start with the *why*. The Engagement Guidelines provide us with strategies to motivate students and also allow them to develop perseverance and coping skills in the classroom. This focus on engagement and autonomy is a cornerstone of UDL and what sets it apart from DI.

# DISCUSSION QUESTIONS

1.  Although UDL and DI share similarities, there are differences between the two frameworks. Imagine someone asks, "They sound the same to me. How are they different?" Practice your answer.

2.  Think about all the teachers, coaches, and bosses you've had in your life. Which one is the most memorable? Reflect on how that person was able to engage you. What are some of the strategies he or she utilized? Bonus points if you can connect those strategies back to the UDL Guidelines.

3.  With your colleagues, create a PD wish list by answering the following questions: What would PD nirvana look like? How would the PD provider build engagement with all learners?

4.  Why is it important to start with *why*?

# Recruiting and Engaging Students as UDL Partners

**4**

Our students, regardless of academic ability, are keenly astute individuals. Sometimes you may feel like your well-planned lessons fall on deaf ears, but your students will always notice if you change the color of your eye shadow, buy a new tie, or wear the same pants two days in a row. Kids pick up more than we realize. Don't believe it? Try this: Allow students to imitate you on the last day of school. Nothing says "I pay attention" like an eerily accurate impersonation of you pushing your hair behind your ear or shuffling papers while you talk. (Note: This is not for the faint of heart.)

Students also may be paying attention to your unintended messages, or your hidden curriculum, instead of your actual lesson. The

**Objective:** *You will learn how to communicate the overall concept of UDL and the Guidelines to students so they can actively help you design and implement your inclusive learning environment.*

**Rationale:** This chapter provides tips on how to explain the UDL Guidelines to students and how to recruit them to be a part of your classroom community. Student understanding of UDL increases their engagement and will save you a lot of time when planning your lessons and setting up your learning environment. It's a win-win situation.

scary thing is that the hidden elements in our learning environment may limit student success more than barriers in the curriculum itself (Anyon, 1980). The books we distribute, the assessments we assign, the way we set up our rooms, and the way we interact with our students all communicate powerful messages. The expressed curriculum—the actual learning materials—may appear rigorous, but how we introduce those materials to students lets them know how we view them.

This concept may be a bit confusing, so here's an analogy to make it more concrete. As adults, we pick up on subtexts all the time. Imagine you tell a friend that you want a Crock-Pot to help you prepare wholesome dinners. The next time that friend gives you a gift, it's a Crock-Pot. This gift is more than an ordinary kitchen appliance. There's a message that goes along with it: "I listen to you. I care about your interests. I support you."

By the same token, when we hand out a book with a 4th-grade reading level to 9th-grade students, we may say, "The content in this book is very mature, so it's perfect for us," but the book itself delivers the real message: "I don't have much faith in your ability to comprehend grade-level material, so I'm going to water it down for you." Now that you know the key difference between UDL and differentiated instruction (DI), you can see that teacher's decisions, even when made with the best intentions, can have unintended effects on students. When students are provided with options and the tools to make those decisions, they hear a very different message.

Three decades ago, Jean Anyon (1980) conducted research in schools that serve different social classes. She discovered that schools educate their students differently by offering curriculum that unintentionally communicates messages about students' worth. The practices that limited students 30 years ago can still impact students today. The difference is that now we know better, so we can work to avoid the same mistakes.

Anyon found that schools that primarily serve populations with low socioeconomic status do not offer students decision-making opportunities. Their job is to follow the directions. Teachers do not explain the importance or significance of any of the curriculum. Above all, teachers insist on following procedures. This type of learning environment informs students that teachers do not expect very much from them. Students hear, "I don't trust you to make decisions. I don't value you enough to share the rationale behind my curriculum. I don't want to hear your voice."

If we offer students a remedial curriculum or run a structured schedule that allows minimal freedom, we are unconsciously preparing our students to aim low. When students are not given freedom of choice or taught critical thinking skills, they are less likely to develop the tools they need to fulfill their career aspirations later in life—whether that is in the professions or the trades or some other path of their choosing. That's not what we want for our kids. Following the UDL Guidelines ensures that we don't communicate these types of hidden messages to our students. When we set the bar high and provide students with options to reach it, it sends them a message that we expect big things from them and we believe in them. That's a lesson they won't soon forget.

Taking it a step further, when we communicate the Guidelines to students, we are saying that we trust them enough to be transparent about our practice. We also give them the power of holding us accountable.

Introducing the concept of UDL to students helps to explain both the importance and the significance of your curriculum. Teaching students about UDL encourages them to make decisions, think critically, and, above all, sends them an important message that you value their input. When designing your lessons, be cognizant of the choices you make and think about what unintended messages students may hear.

To be involved in a UDL learning environment, students have to understand the principles of UDL. Think of it like teaching a cooking class. You could never teach students how to bake chocolate chip cookies unless they first understood that there are a number of necessary ingredients. Think of the Guidelines as your sugar and butter. The more you put in, the better!

Introducing UDL is a great beginning-of-the-year activity, but it can be done any time you are ready to get your students on board. Regardless of the timing, when you're ready to teach your students about UDL, you'll want to translate the Guidelines into accessible language. Provide them with the real language, but work to help them understand the education jargon. But first, it's fun to immerse students in the UDL experience.

One option is to begin class with a traditional lesson and then follow up with a UDL lesson. Whether you work with kindergarten students or adults, this activity is a great example of how different the two learning environments are.

To plan the traditional and UDL lessons, it may be helpful to follow a few steps. Think of them as your recipe for a great learning experience. If you want to plan the lesson your own way, go for it! What follows is just a framework that you may choose to follow or refer to when planning.

## GETTING TO KNOW UDL: THE TRADITIONAL VERSUS THE UDL LESSON

1.  Choose an activity that you would normally give to students that is a total snooze-fest (you know the one!). For example, at the beginning of the school year, elementary school teachers often review class routines while high school teachers and college instructors present students with a syllabus. These beginning-of-the-year activities are great to liven up with some UDL flavor. Just to clarify, the following steps assume you are teaching students about classroom routines, your classroom management system, or your course syllabus (all will be referred to as "routines"), but if you choose to teach another lesson, you can still follow the same process.

2.  Make the most boring, bland copy of the routines you possibly can. (Some of you may find that you don't have to do much work to make it dull. That's fine! It's all part of the process.) If you have a PowerPoint or a Prezi, don't show it. Remove any images from the paper. Make copies with plain text in 12-point font. Your goal here is to bore the students as much as possible. Think of a classroom in the 1950s before technology of any kind. Another option is to have only one copy that you read to the class while they silently listen or take notes.

3. At the beginning of class, distribute the routines and ask students to read silently or begin reading the routines in your best monotone voice. Aspire to sound like the droning teacher from the Charlie Brown shows. Tell students that when the assignment is finished, they will complete an activity about the routines. Just wait a minute and absorb the students' reactions. If it is the beginning of the year, most, if not all, students will be compliant. Glazed over like donuts, but compliant.

4. Once students are "engrossed" in the traditional text, ask them how they are feeling and whether they are enjoying the lesson. Communicate to students that it's okay if they are bored, overwhelmed, or confused by the reading. At this point, encourage students to share their thoughts in one of the following ways. You can have the whole class complete the same reflection activity or give students a choice about which activity they would like to complete. Consider the following options as you start to transition them to UDL.

   • Think-pair-share: To do this, give students a set amount of time to think of an answer. This encourages 100% participation in the next step. Next, pair students together. Finally, ask them to share their answer with a partner. This gets all students talking. Partnering can sometimes be traumatic, and you don't want any students left out, so there are a couple of ways to do this. You can have students count off or ask students to line up based on a certain characteristic (alphabetical order, birth order, and so on) and then pair from there. This gets students out of their seats, which is so important for those who always seem to have the extra energy you so desperately need.

   • Choose a colored Popsicle stick (or index card, marble, or similar) out of a bag and find classmates with the same color. Then, have a group discussion. Randomized grouping is a great way to eliminate the inevitable "I don't have a partner or group" scenario.

- Facilitate a fishbowl discussion where students move chairs into an inner circle and an outer circle. The students in the inner circle discuss how they felt about the lesson while the outer circle listens. Students can switch in and out of the inner circle to say their piece. Another option is to use a "speed dating" protocol where the inner circle sits still while the outer circle rotates every minute or two to discuss the content.

- If students are technologically savvy, ask them to "tweet" their thoughts in writing in fewer than 140 characters. This will get to the main point quickly. Note: Students don't actually need to tweet their thoughts via cell phone, as many school districts may not allow this. Just asking students to write their thoughts in fewer than 140 characters is a fun exercise, especially for the cherubs who are minimalists when it comes to writing. If your school does allow students to BYOD (bring your own device), let them tweet away. Just set up a class hashtag so you can view all the answers on your computer or SMART Board.

- Have students reflect on how they felt in a notebook, in the class journal, or in a drawing. If they choose a drawing, you can have them share their art with the class. If you have a document camera, it's great to project it so the whole class can see it.

After students have had a moment to reflect, explain that the previous lesson was an example of a traditional lesson. If you teach elementary school, you may want to call it the *before lesson* and the UDL lesson the *after lesson*.

## THE UDL LESSON-PLANNING PROCESS

Now it's time to teach your students about your classroom routines by providing them with universally designed options. Before you plan the lesson, the following checklist may help to frame your thinking. This is a list of the questions that I ask myself when I sit down to design learning experiences.

1. Start with the *why*. Specifically, why are you teaching this lesson? Hopefully it's because you want students to achieve an objective or standard. Identify that standard.

2. *Why* do students need to achieve this standard? This will lead you to consider why the knowledge or skill is relevant or valuable to your students.

3. *How* can you assess if students have met or exceeded the standard in a way that is meaningful to them? To ask in another way, *how* will they apply their new knowledge in authentic, valuable ways at the completion of the unit or lesson? When you start a lesson by considering the outcome, it will support you as you plan their learning experiences.

4. After sharing the *why* and *how*, ask students to set a goal for *how* they will persist when the learning becomes difficult, their schedules become too full, or they just don't want to do it. Asking them to set a goal and create a strategy is important for students to build executive function.

5. Next, *what* do students need to know in order to achieve the standard and be successful on the assessment? Can you provide them with options to learn the content or skills?

6. As they are working to learn and apply the content, *how* will they monitor their progress? Consider *how* you will provide mastery oriented feedback so they can deepen their understanding and *how* you will guide them toward mastery?

7. Once the lesson is complete, *how* will you collect feedback from students to foster reflection and to improve future lesson planning?

As you view this "cheat sheet," you may note that the lesson-design practices are the opposite of the way you were taught. When I first started teaching, I started designing lessons by focusing on *what*. I would identify the chapter in the text, the novel, or the lesson I wanted to teach and then think about how students would demonstrate their learning. Finally, I would consider why it was important. I had it all backward.

To return to the Classroom Routines lesson, many teachers would start with the *what*. Although it's important to share what your classroom expectations are, it's critical that students understand why it's important to have classroom expectations in the first place. For example, you may ask students to consider the importance of routines or expectations in general by participating in one or more of the following activities:

- To optimize value and authenticity and activate background knowledge, ask students to consider why different situations in life require different routines and rules. Allow students to work alone or with a partner and choose one of the following situations, or create their own, and list all the "unspoken" rules and routines that are associated with the place or event, and why they are so important. Clearly, depending on the age of your students, some of these options wouldn't be relevant.

  - ❑ Church

  - ❑ Sporting event

  - ❑ Fancy restaurant

  - ❑ Driving

  - ❑ Movie theater

  - ❑ Visiting a grandparent

  - ❑ Attending a birthday party

  - ❑ Getting in an elevator

  - ❑ Playing on the playground

- To foster collaboration and community, and develop reflection, encourage students to share their thoughts about *why* rules, routines, and expectations are important for them and for society in general. Maybe ask them to consider what the world would be like if people didn't follow rules.

As a next step, heighten the salience of goals and objectives by sharing the standard students will be working toward as they learn about the classroom routines. It's up to you as a teacher to determine the area of focus and what you want students to achieve as a result of the learning experience. After students understand *why* rules and routines are important, you want to consider *how* you will assess if they learned the importance of the classroom expectations once you present them. Also, after the lesson, *how* will you assess whether students have an understanding of your expectations in the classroom? Table 4-1 outlines some goals you may want to consider and suggestions for how you could assess students after the lesson by providing them with options.

**TABLE 4-1:** Goals and Assessments: Some Considerations

| GOALS | CONSIDERATIONS FOR AN ASSESSMENT |
|---|---|
| Early Elementary:<br><br>Students write texts to communicate ideas and information to specific audiences for specific purposes. | • Dictate or write a list of the classroom rules and expectations that we could put on the bulletin board using a pencil, colored pencils, or markers.<br><br>• Create an invitation for a new student to come to our classroom. Draw, dictate, or write the rules of the classroom in the invitation.<br><br>• Draw pictures of what the classroom would be like if everyone followed the rules. When you are done, draw a picture of what the classroom would look like if everyone broke the rules. You can share your drawings with your classmates. |

**TABLE 4-1:** Goals and Assessments: Some Considerations  *CONTINUED*

| GOALS | CONSIDERATIONS FOR AN ASSESSMENT |
|---|---|
| Secondary:<br><br>Write informative text that examines a topic, and conveys ideas, concepts, and information, developing the topic with relevant facts, concrete details, and other examples. | Regardless of which option you select, be sure that you use specific information from the classroom expectations and you give examples and provide details about what the classroom will be like if we follow or don't follow the expectations.<br><br>• Write a catchy poem or song about the importance of following our classroom routines. (You can sing it at presentation time!)<br><br>• In your journal, write about our classroom routines and why it is important that we all follow them.<br><br>• Create a handout to give to students about the classroom rules and routines.<br><br>• Imagine you are designing a social media site about our classroom rules (e.g., Twitter, Facebook, Vine). Create at least five posts that share our classroom routines and demonstrate the importance of them.<br><br>• Write a skit about classroom rules using dialogue and stage directions, and then act it out live or on video.<br><br>• Super Challenge: Write a letter to the principal, noting classroom rules and routines that should be in every classroom in the school and why this consistency is important. Be sure to use formal language appropriate for the principal. |

As you begin to build your student handout, you may want to use the template outlined in the "Our Classroom Routines" section as an exemplar. Note that there is an objective on the top of the page, a rationale for the assignment, choices for how students will express their knowledge, and coping strategies if they get frustrated. One common complaint of giving students choices is that some students will spend too long trying to decide which assignment to pick. One quick way to fix this is to provide six options, the seventh being "Roll the dice." If students have not chosen an assignment within 2 minutes, they must roll the dice. Some students will always choose this option just to try their luck. If six choices is too many, younger students may have only two choices with the option to flip a coin. It's completely up to you!

---

## ✔ Our Classroom Routines

**Objective:** *Write informative text that examines a topic and conveys ideas, concepts, and information, developing the topic with relevant facts, concrete details, and other examples.*

**Rationale:** To minimize distractions in the classroom so we can learn, everyone has to follow the classroom rules and routines. I want to make sure you understand the routines so we can all learn as much as possible this year. Complete one of the following assignments to express your understanding of our routines.

### Choose Your Assignment

You can work alone or with a partner.

1.  Write a catchy poem or song about the importance of following our classroom routines. (You can sing it at presentation time!)

---

2. In your journal, write about our classroom routines and why it is important that we all follow them.

3. Create a handout to give to students about the classroom rules and routines.

4. Imagine you are designing a social media site about our classroom rules (Twitter, Facebook, Vine). Create at least 5 posts that share our classroom routines and demonstrate the importance of them.

5. Write a skit about classroom rules using dialogue and stage directions and then act it out live or on video.

6. Super Challenge: Write a letter to the principal, noting classroom rules and routines that should be in every classroom in the school and why this consistency is important. Be sure to use formal language appropriate for the principal.

7. Roll the dice! The only rule is you must respect the dice. Whatever you roll, you have to do.

## Scaffolding (for older students)

If you get frustrated while working, follow this procedure:

1. Read the assignment guidelines again.

2. Write down the questions that you have about the assignment or highlight the specific directions that are confusing to you.

3. Ask your partner or someone around you for help. Have them write their suggestions or answers on your paper. If they don't know, have them write why they are also confused.

4. If this doesn't help, raise your hand to get my attention. I will read your questions and your classmate's feedback to try to help you.

After you determine the *why* and the *how*, you can begin to plan your lesson as you share your classroom expectations with students so they know what your expectations are. The Representation Guidelines will support you as you plan for the *what*. The "cheat sheet" further clarifies the considerations inherent in those Guidelines.

## ▶ Representation Cheat Sheet

When planning a lesson:

1. State the standard or objective

2. Pre-teach or provide options for students to focus on important vocabulary, key terms, or symbols that will be important for comprehension.

3. Activate prior knowledge: remind students what they already know about the content.

4. Create a visual component (Ask yourself, how would a student who is deaf access this material?). Also have a digital copy of the lesson so students can access if necessary on iPad or laptop.

5. Create an audio component (Ask yourself, how would a student who is visually impaired access the material?).

6. Use technology options to engage students.

After you present your lesson, students will then apply their newly acquired knowledge using the assessment you designed at the beginning of the lesson planning process. To develop self-assessment and bring engagement full circle, ask students to reflect on their performance and their effort once they complete their assessment by participating in options for reflection. For example, you may provide options to students to foster reflection in one of the following ways.

1.  Write a personal reflection on how you felt about completing the traditional lesson verses the UDL lesson.

2.  Assign a grade to your assignment and explain why you earned that grade.

3.  Using pipe cleaners or Play-Doh, sculpt a representation about how you felt about your work on the assignment. When finished, you can present the sculptures to the class.

4.  Put out a pile of different, random objects (stickers, post cards, toys, temporary tattoos) and ask students to choose one and explain why it represents how they felt about the UDL lesson.

5.  Fill out a reflection sheet like the one below. If you teach younger students, you can just use the emoticons, while older students can use the letter grades.

Grade yourself on the following sheet:

| | A | B | C | D | F |
|---|---|---|---|---|---|
| How hard did you work today? | | | | | |
| How much did you enjoy the lesson today? | | | | | |
| How well do you understand the classroom routines and rules? | | | | | |

Now it's time to introduce the concept of UDL. You can use one of the following scripts to introduce the concept to your students. If you choose to read the script to the class, have a printed copy and a projected copy available for students who prefer to learn visually.

**Pre-K - Early Elementary script** All of you are different and special in your own way. Because of that, you all learn in different ways. To help you learn, I'm going to give you choices so you can pick activities that will be the best for you. When I give you choices, don't worry about what your friends are picking because all your brains are different and you need different things to stay interested and work your hardest. I'm going to give you a choice now so you can see how different you are. Pretend that we are going to do an art project. Would you rather color with crayons or markers, make something out of clay, paint on an easel, or draw outside on the sidewalk? [Allow students to share their answers and/or get into groups based on their preference]. Now, wouldn't it be boring if you didn't ever get to make any choices? That won't happen because I'm going to work really hard to give you choices every day!

**Elementary script** This year I have to teach certain things, some of which will be really challenging for some of you. To make sure that all of you do really well, I'm going to plan lessons that will help all of you learn. For example, some of you may love reading books while others learn better when they listen to a story. You may even change the way you like to learn from day to day! Whenever I plan lessons, I'm going to use something called Universal Design for Learning. When something is universal, it means that everyone in the whole world can use it. I'm going to try to make some of my lessons universal so you will all be able to show me what you've learned in different ways.

**Secondary script** This year I am required to teach a number of curriculum standards. In order to insure that you meet and/or exceed those standards, I will spend a lot of time designing the curriculum to give you the best chance to succeed. I want you know that when you walk into this classroom, I have spent a lot of time preparing and aligning my curriculum to the principles of Universal Design for Learning, or UDL for short. UDL accounts for the fact that that all of you are different in so many ways. Since you all have different interests and learn in various ways, I'll create lessons that keep you engaged. You'll hear me reference UDL a lot throughout the year, so I want you to know a little about it right from the start.

Once students have a general understanding of UDL and have reflected on the lesson, you have an opportunity to facilitate a class discussion to collect students' first impressions and feedback about UDL. Next, you can segue into a survey to collect information about students' learning preferences and interests. The results of this activity will prove learner variability, helping both you and the class see that everyone learns differently.

If you hand out a survey to students, help them to understand that you will use the information to ensure that all their needs are met throughout the year. This is a great activity to get to know students, so if you already distribute a getting-to-know-you survey, just add some UDL learning inventory questions to it. Also, before asking the students to answer the questions, it's good practice to provide an exemplar and fill out the survey yourself. Some students may feel embarrassed about their interests or perceived weaknesses in the classroom, but if you discuss how you learn best in certain situations, it will minimize the threat of students not being truthful about perceived flaws. As adults, we all have characteristics that act as barriers when we try to learn new information in specific settings, and students need to know they aren't alone. For example, my learning "kryptonite" is that I need to see something to learn it when I'm in a classroom. If I'm asked to listen, I'll zone out, but give me something to read, and I'm in! Interestingly, if I am cooking, I would prefer not to read recipes. Instead, I prefer to watch *Top Chef* and follow along.

That being said, it's important not to use student responses to label them. All learners vary greatly in their learning preferences based on task and setting, and it's powerful when students can understand that.

Helping students feel capable and comfortable the way they are is a great way to start the year. When presenting learning inventory questions, consider allowing students to fill out a paper copy, respond orally in small groups, or access the survey on an online survey tool.

# TEACHING STUDENTS ABOUT THE GUIDELINES

After teaching students about the general concept of UDL and reflecting on the process, share the individual Guidelines with them so they begin to understand curriculum design and how much thought and effort goes into your UDL lessons. If you're wondering why this is necessary, just remember Anyon's study on hidden curriculum. Students will pick up on the fact that you are including them in the learning process, and this tells students more than your curriculum ever will. If you have older students, you may want to provide them with a copy of the actual UDL Guidelines for educators (Figure 2-2) and encourage them to use highlighters or take notes while you are translating the Guidelines for them, if it would be helpful.

## Engagement Guidelines

Begin by explaining that the Guidelines are divided into three sections: the Engagement Guidelines, the Representation Guidelines, and the Action and Expression Guidelines. If you think it would be interesting to your students, you may want to delve into the brain research a little, as well. You could give students a template of a brain and have them color it. If you teach science, you could ask them to label other parts of the brain as they work. The possibilities are endless.

A kindergarten teacher in my district started off the school year by asking her students to make "brain puppets." She provided students with a handout of the UDL brain and encouraged them to color the different networks of the brain. As they colored, she explained that three parts of the brain were responsible for learning and it was her job to "light up" all three parts of their brains so they could learn. It was neuroscience for five-year-olds!

If you choose to share the Guidelines with your students, you could spend a couple of days introducing the UDL Guidelines, or you could introduce one Guideline a day until you've covered them all. Each time you introduce a Guideline, give it a place of permanence in your classroom on a bulletin board or in student binders. This will keep you accountable all year and remind students how you value each of them and appreciate their individuality.

For each UDL Guideline that follows, you will find simplified language for elementary and secondary students and tips for how to involve students in your learning environment with a focus on each Guideline. You know your students better than anyone, so as you're reading, think about which suggestions you could implement in your classroom. Remember, the more you involve students in creating a learning environment that includes UDL principles, the easier it will be for you to design your lessons and fully implement a UDL curriculum. Taking some of the following suggestions and turning them into routines will save you countless hours throughout the year. (Also, for those readers familiar with the numbered version of the Guidelines [Figure 2-1], I've noted the Guideline numbers in the following charts to help ease your transition.)

The Engagement Guidelines relate to engaging students or making the content interesting or relevant to the students. The Guidelines also allow you to foster perseverance and a growth mindset in students when learning is challenging. These Guidelines tend to interest students the most because frankly the Guidelines are all about them, and how they cope when frustrated, bored, or anxious.

## Provide Options for Self-Regulation

This was previously Guideline 9.

|  |  |
|---|---|
|  | Promote expectations and beliefs that optimize motivation. Facilitate personal coping skills and strategies. Develop self-assessment and reflection. |
| Elementary translation | This year, my job is to help you learn a lot of new information, but I also want to teach you how to do your own work. When you get older, you'll have to complete a lot of work on your own, but it's important to learn how to do that. Throughout the year, I will teach you different strategies that will help you complete your work even when it seems really hard and it would be easier to give up. |

| Secondary translation | To be successful in college or in your chosen career, you have to learn how to push yourself to do your best work even when there is no one around to assess you. In prior years, teacher feedback was probably your sole source of assessment, but now that you're getting older, it's important that you learn how to assess your own work and persist despite obstacles. In life, your boss won't show the same patience your teachers do so this year we will focus on strategies to keep you motivated even when work seems too difficult. |
|---|---|

Here are some concrete strategies to implement into your learning environment to help students self-regulate:

❑ Have students complete a self-reflection after teaching each standard to get feedback on how well your lesson went. Here is an example that could be used.

| | A | B | C | D | F |
|---|---|---|---|---|---|
| Determine a theme or central idea of a text and analyze its development over the course of the text. | | | | | |
| Compare and contrast texts in different forms or genres (e.g., stories and poems; historical novels and fantasy stories) in terms of their approaches to similar themes and topics. | | | | | |

When you are finished, answer one of the following questions:

1. Did the lesson help you to meet the standard? If not, what was confusing about the lesson?

2. What could you have done better today?

3. What could I, as your teacher, have done better today?

4. Did you enjoy today's lesson? Why or why not?

Here are some concrete strategies to help students self-regulate:

❑ Teach students about coping skills. For example, many students will get frustrated and give up, but there are many ways to keep working despite obstacles. It may be helpful to teach students about relaxation techniques or Mandala coloring. You may also set up an area of the classroom with stress balls or other manipulatives that students can use when they get frustrated.

❑ Teach students how to block their time and reward themselves for meeting mini-deadlines. Model this for them and explain how you manage your time when planning lessons. Setting a timer is very helpful for some students.

❑ Teach them about Zentangle (www.zentangle.com), a therapeutic doodling activity that helps students to relax. Allow them to Zentangle or color after meeting specific deadlines or working for a specific amount of time. This will help them with time management and will teach them strategies they can use when they are working on their homework.

## Provide Options for Sustaining Effort and Persistence

This was previously Guideline 8.

| | |
|---|---|
| | Heighten salience of goals and objectives. |
| | Vary demands and resources to optimize challenge. |
| | Foster collaboration and communication. |
| | Increase mastery-oriented feedback. |
| Elementary translation | At the beginning of every assignment, I will always explain what we are about to do and why it's important that you learn it. Also, I will try really hard to give you choices of assignments so you can pick the one that is not too easy or too hard (you can make a reference to *Goldilocks and the Three Bears*). Sometimes, I'll also let you work with partners or in groups so when work seems hard, you can ask someone for help. I'll always be available for help, too, so don't be afraid to pick a difficult assignment. |

| Secondary translation | How many of you have ever asked a teacher, "What are we doing today?" That's because as learners, we want to know what the goal is. None of us wants to complete an assignment if we don't know what the point is, right? That's why throughout the year we're going to focus on what we are learning and why we are learning it. Also, to keep you motivated, you will have many opportunities to choose your assignment so you can pick something that appropriately challenges you. To push yourself to do your best work, I will always encourage you to choose something just out of your comfort zone, but then I will allow you to collaborate and will give feedback to help you achieve. |
|---|---|

Here are some concrete strategies to implement in your learning environment to help students sustain effort and persistence:

- ❑ Whether you have an online learning management system (LMS), chart paper, a white board, or a high-tech SMART Board, you should have a plan for the day mapped out for the students and any roaming administrators to see. In addition to posting on the agenda board, it's valuable to make copies for students who aren't in class so the next day they can see what they missed. You can staple any handouts to the agenda for them. If you are an elementary school teacher, you teach too many subjects to realistically write detailed agendas for each subject, so instead you may want to create a schedule for the day and write the main standard for each subject. This will allow students to see how their day will go and the main content they will study.

- ❑ If you have an LMS or a class webpage, you could take a picture of your agenda board every day and post it online. If you have different colored chalk or markers, you could make it a work of art, or you could give students markers and ask them to decorate the agenda or draw a decorative border. Once you take a picture, you have a record every day. If you fear you'll forget to take the picture each day, you could assign a class photographer.

❑ Have a student in your homeroom or first period write the agenda every morning. Many students would love to have the opportunity to write on the board. They could also decorate it at this time if you allow.

❑ Once you put up the agenda, you could have one student copy it down for students who are absent. That "bookkeeper" could also write notes to the classmate during the class that would aid comprehension. This responsibility sometimes adds extra focus.

❑ One important thing you can do to set up a UDL classroom is to take the time to read your curriculum standards and simplify the language so the whole educational team understands them. Once you have done this, you shouldn't just put this list in your desk. It should wallpaper your classroom, your bulletin boards, your planning book, and student binders. If everyone has a copy of the standards, it keeps you accountable. Your gut reaction may be that this may show weakness if you don't get to a standard, but I promise you, if it's posted, you'll get to it. It keeps you on task so much more than if it's in a book in your desk. Every time you complete a standard, highlight it or check it off so you know it's been covered. If you have older students, you can give them a copy and have them do the same. It really gives them a sense of accomplishment to cross things off.

❑ One cool way to post standards is to assign one standard to each student and have him or her write it neatly with different colored markers. Then, they could personalize it by designing a border. If you already have the standards written, you could just tack the standard up every day instead of rewriting it on the white board. Try to have the standard on the top of each assignment as well. If your school ever goes to standards-based reporting or if you're already there, it will make grading much easier.

❑ Post a to-do list for extended assignments or for multiple assignments. For example, "Citing textual evidence" is an important literacy standard. As a result, when I taught 7th grade, I aimed for 20 text-based responses a year. On my bulletin board, I had a countdown of open responses, and every time we completed one, we crossed it off. The second I handed one out, students were on me to log it in, and then someone would inevitably shout, "Wow, only 17 left!" How many of you like to write to-do lists and cross things off? It's the same thing for kids. It also teaches a great organizational strategy. It helps them to realize that they are working toward a goal.

## Provide Options for Recruiting Interest

This was previously Guideline 7.

| | Optimize individual choice and autonomy. Optimize relevance, value, and authenticity. Minimize threats and distractions. |
|---|---|
| Elementary translation | We all are very different and have many different interests. Because we are so different, we probably don't all want to complete the same assignments all the time. To try to make everyone happy, there will be times when you'll get to choose from many assignments so you can find something that is interesting to you. |
| Secondary translation | People are very different in how they learn. This is the rule, not the exception. So, it's important for educators to provide different assignment options so all students can be engaged in the learning process at their appropriate level of challenge. |

Here are some concrete strategies to implement into your learning environment to help recruit students' interest:

- ❏ If you want to minimize threats and distractions in the classroom, you need students to be respectful. One way to do this is to write a class pledge. In one class I observed in a high-poverty district in Massachusetts, the pledge read, "I promise to treat others with respect and courtesy, to make responsible decisions, and to be accountable for my actions. I believe I can succeed. I believe I can make a difference in my community. I will try every day to let my character shine and use my power for good." You could write a similar pledge in your classroom.

- ❏ In order to know what interests your students, you have to know them. It's not enough that you know what their learning preferences are or you know what assignments they like best. You should also know the sports they play, what music they like, and what talents they have. Students are human beings just like us, and they need to know that people care about them and understand them. Take some time at the beginning of the year to survey students about their interests, ask students to make a presentation about who they are, or just spend one minute a day talking to a different student.

- ❏ One fun way to learn about students, regardless of what subject you teach, is to ask them to write you a letter or e-mail explaining why they should be your favorite student. See the prompt below that you can use or adapt. As mentioned previously, it's always good to give students an exemplar, so draft a letter yourself, arguing why you should be their favorite teacher. Make sure you note that one reason is because you rock at UDL!

- ❏ Ask students to watch the news, listen to the radio, or read a magazine and identify aspects that relate to your content. Encourage them to share connections with the class.

# ▶ Who Is My Favorite?

Argument writing is writing that attempts to convince the reader to adopt a particular opinion. I know that all of you are very good at argument, even if you don't know it yet. That is why you are going to argue why you should be my favorite student. I have many students, so you must be very convincing. Follow these steps to brainstorm some reasons why you should be my favorite:

1. Think of things that you could present to me that would make me happy. Does your mom bake a great cake? Does your uncle have a dog-sitting service? Could you walk my dog for me? Are you really good at washing cars? Make sure that you are honest and only list things that you would be able to do. (You do not really have to do any of these things; you're just thinking about resources you have.) Be very creative because I'm sure that all of you are wonderful at so many things. Please dictate, draw, or write at least **three** things that you could do for me to get the Favorite Student Award.

2. Next, think about the way that you act in class. What part of your behavior would make me happy? Are you excellent at drawing, reading, or writing? Are you quiet when I am talking? Would you tell jokes to make me laugh? Dictate, draw, or write down at least **three** things you could do in class that would make you my favorite.

3. Last, think about all the really cool things you can do. Can you shoot three-pointers, solve a Rubix cube, do a back-flip, play the violin, or eat saltines with no water? Write down **three** things that make you unique and would totally impress me.

4. Now you are ready to share why you should be my favorite student. Be sure to include at least five of the previous ideas in your letter. (You brainstormed nine, so you are getting off easy!) You can use as many as you'd like, but only five are required.

5. Determine how you will present me with your information. You have the following options:

   a. For younger students:

      • Draw detailed pictures of all the reasons why you should be my favorite student. Write or dictate captions for each picture.

      • Bring in two show-and-tell items that will show me why you should be my favorite student. Write or dictate why each item shows why you should be my favorite student.

   b. For older students:

      • You can write me a letter, email, poem or song about why you should be my favorite student.

      • Create a blog that you will share with the world, or just me, about why you should be my favorite student.

      • Produce a commercial and record using video or audio so you can present how you will be my favorite student.

## Representation Guidelines

The Representation Guidelines focus on how you will present information to students. Some students, especially older ones, may have had teachers who presented information using one primary method, such as reading or lecturing. Explain that you will make an effort to vary your presentation methods to keep them on their toes.

## Provide Options for Comprehension

This was previously Guideline 3.

|  | Activate or supply background knowledge.<br><br>Highlight patterns, critical features, big ideas, and relationships.<br><br>Guide information processing, visualization, and manipulation.<br><br>Maximize generalization and transfer. |
| --- | --- |
| Elementary translation | It's easier to learn something new when you can relate it to something you already know. Before we begin new lessons, we'll work together to figure out what we already know about the subject. When we finish learning a new topic, we will talk about how it we can use that new knowledge in different ways. |
| Secondary translation | Before learning new academic content, it's important to activate your prior knowledge of similar content. This practice will allow your brain to compartmentalize the new information so you understand it better. We will work all year to make and visualize important connections before and after each lesson so you will be able to see the relationships between everything you are learning. |

Here are some concrete strategies to implement into your learning environment to improve the comprehension of all students:

❑ Visualization is an important skill for students, but many do not do this naturally. This is another opportunity to call on class artists to draw concrete connections so other learners can see relationships between ideas. Ask students to come up to the white board or chart paper to sketch visual representations or graphic organizers to explain how new content fits into what students already know. Students always love to see their peers' artwork, especially when it's done in real time.

❑ KWL charts encourage students to think about what they already know about a topic before moving on with a lesson. In a simple KWL chart like the following one, students identify what they already know about a topic and what they want to know. After the lesson is completed, they can enter what they have learned.

| WHAT I ALREADY KNOW | WHAT I WANT TO KNOW | WHAT I LEARNED |
|---|---|---|
| | | |

If individual students complete a chart like this before a lesson begins, they can share their prior knowledge with other students. Another option is to complete the KWL chart as a class so you have a sense of the collective prior knowledge of the group.

## Provide Options for Language, Mathematical Expressions, and Symbols

This was previously Guideline 2.

| | |
|---|---|
| | Clarify vocabulary and symbols. |
| | Clarify syntax and structure. |
| | Support decoding of text, mathematical notation, and symbols. |
| | Promote understanding across languages. |
| | Illustrate through multiple media. |
| Elementary translation | In order to make a cake, you have to follow a recipe. Recipes have lots of symbols and words. If you don't know all the symbols or words, you won't make a very tasty cake. In order to do well in school, you have to know symbols as well, like numbers and letters. This year, whenever we come to a new symbol or structure, we will spend time learning about it and using it so you will be able to use that symbol when you are doing work on your own. |

| Secondary translation | Academic vocabulary is important for college and/or your chosen career. To help you access academic vocabulary, I'll pre-teach important concepts and provide graphics that will help you remember and own the new words. There are formulas at work in almost everything you'll learn about this year. Solving mathematical equations, identifying text structures, and writing essays are all complex processes with concrete steps. Regardless of what we're learning, I'll make sure to highlight the different components for you so you can be successful when you have to complete the work independently. |
| --- | --- |

Here are some concrete strategies to implement in your learning environment to help all students learn important expressions and symbols:

❏ Ask students to bring manipulatives from home, find images online or in a magazine, or even draw images for upcoming vocabulary words. They can share these visual supports with their classmates.

❏ In order for students to understand important domain-specific symbols, they have to know that symbols take ordinary objects and attach meaning that is much deeper. A fun way to kick this off is to ask each student to develop their own symbol and present it to the class. Prompt them to think about favorite hobbies, sports, or favorite items; important events in their lives; and characteristics that are important to them (courage, loyalty, sense of humor). The symbol must represent who they are without including their names. You can hang the symbols in the classroom and refer to them throughout the year whenever you teach a new symbol.

❏ Create a bulletin board in class that will include vocabulary words you teach throughout the year. Whenever there is a new word, a different student can write the word and a graphic symbol to help classmates remember it and post it on the board. In this way, vocabulary is accessible every day and students can see how many new words they have learned. You could allow students to write the word in any font, color, size, and so on, as long as it is legible. If you teach younger grades, you could write the word and let students color the letters or trace them, or draw pictures.

## Provide Options for Perception

This was previously Guideline 1.

|  | Offer ways of customizing the display of information.<br><br>Offer alternatives for auditory information.<br><br>Offer alternatives for visual information. |
| --- | --- |
| Elementary translation | I will try very hard to make sure that when I teach lessons, I have something for you to look at and something for you to listen to. Also, I'm going to type many assignments on the computer, so if you have a hard time reading the papers I hand out, you can use one of the computers to make the letters or pictures bigger, change the color, or have the computer read it to you. |
| Secondary translation | I will make every effort to ensure that I supplement reading material with visuals and technology. Also, I will post class handouts and assignment guidelines on my class webpage or in our LMS so you can download them to your computer, tablet, or smart phone. Our textbook is online, as well, so you can customize the font, and even better, you won't ever forget your work at school. Lastly, whenever there is an assignment, I will provide written guidelines, but I will also explain the directions aloud and check in to ensure comprehension. |

Here are some concrete strategies to implement into your learning environment so you are providing options for all students to perceive curriculum materials:

- ❑ Post a job application for class "techs," the kids who seem to know more than you about technology. Once you have their applications, submitted in writing or orally, you can assign students certain jobs. For example, maybe you have an iPad expert who can tutor classmates on how to access information online. There are probably many kindergarteners who can change the preferences on an iPad or computer. If they are elementary students, they may enjoy little nametags. After all, they are important "employees" who should be recognized for their valuable contributions. If you teach older students, you could use a generic job application to give them practice in filling out a real one.

- ❑ If you teach older students and have proficient typists, ask for student volunteers who would be willing to type copies of assignments you only have in hard copy. This is especially great for students who always seem to be finished early (you know who they are!). Many students excel at this and even add graphics and headings that are more impressive than your original files.

- ❑ Many teachers already assign class jobs, but another way to do this is to post a "Board of Operations" in the classroom. On my 7th-grade team in Chelmsford, we assigned four jobs: the administrative assistant, the facilities manager, the distributor, and the bookkeeper. The administrative assistant handled day-to-day errands, troubleshooting of technology, and so on. The facilities manager made sure all students cleaned up after themselves before they left class. The distributor handed out papers. The bookkeeper took important notes for students who were absent, poor note-takers, or not auditory learners. You could customize this list to add a tech job or an artist job. You could change jobs weekly, once a month, or once a quarter.

❑ To help to keep your class organized, buy plastic shoe organizers to keep student work. In the front of the room, you can mount the shoe organizers on the bulletin board. In each pocket, place a colorful nametag for each student, and behind the nametag put all the handouts for the class period and all corrected work. As the students file into class, they can stop at the bulletin board, grab their work, and sit down. No class time is lost handing out papers. You can ask a student to distribute the papers into the organizers for you in the previous class or during homeroom.

❑ Survey students to identify the best artists in class. Whenever you're reading or lecturing, one of the artists can draw images on the white board, on chart paper, or under a document camera so other students can visualize what is happening. Not only does it help you with the Representation Guidelines, but it's engaging for other students.

❑ Have volunteers take notes during lectures on a laptop and post them to the class webpage for printing and downloading. If you have a projector, another option is to have a student type notes on your computer so students who have a difficult time accessing the auditory information can read the notes in real time. If you don't have a computer in the classroom, a note-taker can write the notes on a white board, blackboard, overhead projector, or in their notebooks, and then you can make copies.

❑ Another option is to ask someone in your class to take visual notes, or sketch notes. Sketch notes allow note takers to make sense of complex content by offering visual information that highlights patterns, critical features, big ideas, and relationships in a critical context.

❑ As an enrichment activity, have students bring in images or manipulatives that are relevant to the content area. Think of it as a beefed-up show-and-tell. If you have a choice of content, survey students to find out what is most interesting to them so they are more likely to have items to bring in. For example, even your most reluctant student would probably be flattered to demonstrate how to dribble a basketball, show off pictures of their uncle's tricked-out truck, or show off a scar they got biking.

❑ For stories or text without an audio component, have your best readers read the story aloud into a voice recorder. Once you have the MP3 file, you can play it back for students who would benefit from it. You can also post this recording online so students can download it to their devices. Some students will even go the extra mile and add accents. That's always a treat!

# Expression Guidelines

Once you have taught curricular content to students, they have to express their knowledge back to you. Explain to students that you'll have many practices in place to ensure that they can be successful in this task.

## Provide Options for Executive Functions

This was previously Guideline 6.

| | |
|---|---|
| | Guide appropriate goal-setting. |
| | Support planning and strategy development. |
| | Facilitate managing information and resources. |
| | Enhance capacity for monitoring progress. |
| Elementary translation | Throughout the year you will be expected to do more and more work on your own. To help you do this, I will give you a number of different supports. For every assignment, I will give you the option to view an example of what the finished product may look like, and I will provide you with all the steps you need to be successful as you complete an assignment. This will help you to complete many assignments on your own. |
| Secondary translation | There are [however many] of you and one of me. You are therefore your own best resource when it comes to completing your assignments. I will do my job and supply with you assignment objectives, exemplars, rubrics, and strategies for completing assignments, and I will also teach you strategies so you can be your own best teacher. |

Here are some concrete strategies to implement into your learning environment to explicitly teach executive functions:

❑ In order to build executive function skills, students need the opportunity to set their own goals and create their own strategy. An important part of creating a strategy is determining what information and resources you need to be successful and also how you're going to monitor your progress. To begin this work, ask students to create a personal goal for the month. For example, maybe they want to shoot a three pointer in basketball, learn to tie their shoes, audition for the school play, save up to buy a guitar, etc ... Once students write their goal, have them create a strategy, or a to-do list, so they know the steps they will have to take to achieve their goal. Help them to see that this strategy includes "managing information and resources" because a student cannot shoot a three pointer in basketball, for example, without access to a hoop, a ball, and some way to measure the three point line. If you teach younger students, you could complete this activity as a class. An example follows:

❑ *Goal: Shoot 75% from the free throw line by December.*

❑ *Find out how many feet away the free throw line is*

❑ *Get a measuring tape and measure how far away it is*

❑ *Make a mark so I know where the line is*

❑ *Ask dad if he will paint a line on the drive way*

❑ *If he says yes, help him paint the line (maybe have to buy paint)*

❑ *If he says no, ask him to buy tape or chalk*

❑ *Ask dad to paint or tape the line*

❑ *Shoot 100 free throws every day after school*

❑ *On Friday, write down how many of 100 I got in [and so on]*

❑ Once students understand how to create a strategy that aligns to their goals, ask them to begin to use this executive function for assessments. After you share the goal or objective and the options for assessments, students can select their own goal and begin to build a strategy so they can achieve it.

- ❑ *Goal: Make a book to teach first graders about a dinosaur.*

- ❑ *Pick my favorite dinosaur*

- ❑ *Go to library on Monday and take out 3 books on dinosaurs*

- ❑ *Write down three facts about my dinosaur from each book*

- ❑ *Get everything I need to make a book like paper, colored pencils and markers*

- ❑ *Write all the facts on the bottom of the pages from my notes in pencil*

- ❑ *Go over the words in marker [and so on]*

❑ If you have younger students, you may find it easier to create these strategies as a class, so you build collective efficacy in your classroom. I recently observed a second grade teacher who sat with her class before an assessment so all the students could brainstorm all the steps they would need to take to be successful as they completed a task and all the materials they should have on their desks before they began. If you provide students with a everything they need, they don't have the opportunity to practice these skills.

❑ It's important to supply students with the option to view work exemplars for every assignment. This prevents the inevitable, "I couldn't do it because I didn't know what I was supposed to do." When you give students a sample of what you're looking for, it answers a lot of the questions they have about completing the assignment. You may be wondering, "Where will I get these sample assignments if I've never assigned them before?" When it comes to exemplars, you have a choice: you can either complete an example yourself or ask a student to use his or her work as an exemplar. Completing them yourself may seem like a pretty big commitment, but remember, you're the expert in the room and it's important for students to see master work. This is not, however, the only option. Involving kids in creating these exemplars is valuable, too. It is a great enrichment activity for students who need an extra challenge. If you know that one of your students exceeds one of your standards, ask him or her to complete a future assignment that aligns to that standard. Tell him or her that you would love to use his or her work as an exemplar for other students. The flattery alone will make most students jump at the chance. Another option is after an assignment is complete, take the best exemplar and share it with the class. Then, you can have other students revise their assignments to improve them. This process of revision is an important skill that students can transfer to other classes and assignments.

❏ For an assignment early in the year, encourage students to think of a complex process they know a lot about. Encourage them to break down the process into simple steps and then write the process, perform a skit, or give a live or multimedia presentation. For example, a golf swing looks like one simple movement, but it's actually made up of many complex steps. The same is true for processes such as blowing and popping a bubble of gum, sending a text, tying a shoe, and so on. Explain after the presentation that your assignments will follow this same process. Whether students complete a lab report, solve an algebraic equation, swing a baseball bat, or write a paragraph, they need to know there are many steps to follow to be successful.

## Provide Options for Expression and Communication

This was previously Guideline 5.

|  | Use multiple media for communication. |
|  | Use multiple tools for construction and composition. |
|  | Build fluencies with graduated levels of support for practice and performance. |

| Elementary translation | This will not be a class where we only take multiple-choice tests at the end of every unit. I want everyone to feel comfortable performing skits, making posters, and playing learning games. After we learn a new skill, you will have a number of choices about how you will express your knowledge to me. |
|---|---|
| Secondary translation | Taking multiple-choice tests and writing essays are important skills, but there are many other ways for students to express knowledge that can be even more challenging. In this class, there will be an expectation that you push yourself to try new and varied methods to express knowledge, creativity, and your presentation abilities. All three of these actions will help you to be successful in college or in your chosen career. |

Here are some concrete strategies to implement into your learning environment that will allow you to provide multiple ways for students to express their knowledge and skills:

❏ At the beginning of the year, ask students to help you make a creative idea bank with many different assignment options. If you can generate a long list of possible assignments (such as skits, songs, dances, Animotos, PowerPoints, and so on), it will make your life a lot easier when you need to come up with assignment choices. There is a long list of assignment options in Chapter 7, but students are always on the receiving end of new technology, so they will probably have better ideas than any of us could come up with. Students, especially older ones, are sometimes more technologically savvy than their teachers, so pick their brains to ask what type of assignments they like to complete. You could also take this to the next level and write the assignment ideas on index cards and laminate them. Whenever students have a choice about which assignment to choose, they could reach into the grab bag to try their luck. The element of chance will engage some students immediately.

❑ If possible, try to get different materials in the classroom for students to use when completing assignments. Most teachers prefer blue or black ink, but allowing students to use your special purple sparkly pens will literally get some of them to write when they would not have otherwise. Having special markers, pens, sparkles, and so on, that students can use when working on assignments increases the excitement. You have to let go of the control of the assignment a little, but it's worth it to see the students excited about communicating their knowledge to you. You can even ask students to bring in materials from home if possible. I had one student who completed a full essay on a napkin because he thought it was funny. He received an A (Figure 4-1).

❑ Just changing things up and allowing students to complete assignments in unique ways will engage them and allow them to express their knowledge to you.

**FIGURE 4-1:** Fabulous napkin assessment

## Provide Options for Physical Action

This was previously Guideline 4.

| | Vary the methods for response and navigation. |
|---|---|
| | Optimize access to tools and assistive technologies. |
| Elementary translation | If you don't have very good eyesight, you need to wear glasses. This is an accommodation that helps you learn. There are many other accommodations that help people learn, like typing, using joysticks, or using special software on the computer. I will always allow and encourage you to use the resources that help you learn the best. |
| Secondary translation | We live in a world where technology reigns supreme. To keep up with the times, we must keep up with technology. Therefore, I will allow you to type any and all assignments or use any accommodations on the computer that will help you to express your ideas, such as voice-recognition software, spellcheck, and so on. (Note to teachers: If you have a specific classroom policy about using technology on assignments, you can insert that here.) |

Here are some concrete strategies to implement into your learning environment to help you provide options for physical action:

❑ If you have students who use specific technology to help complete assignments, have them demonstrate how to use it with other students. Some students use speech recognition software or reading software like WordQ. These applications are amazing resources that all students should have access to at some point. When all students have the option to experiment with such technologies, the tools lose the stigma of being for special education students.

❑ If your kids are very tech-savvy, you could have a technology show-and-tell once a week or once a month where you have students come up and show classmates how to access different apps and websites that help them in the content area. Even if your school is not a BYOD school, you may get permission to allow students to bring in their devices for the show-and-tell.

# SUMMARY

At the beginning of the chapter, you learned about the hidden curriculum and the message it sends to students. You may not be able to fix the hidden messages communicated in your school, but you certainly have the power to change the messages in your learning environment. UDL will help you to do that.

One important aspect of UDL is engaging students, and the best way to do that is by involving them. You may be feeling skeptical about opening up your curriculum-design process to students, but if you do, you are sending them an important message: that you value them and their opinions. Also, the more you involve them, the more involved they will be, and the closer you will be to full UDL implementation. It's something you just have to try because it will change your practice and your students.

# DISCUSSION QUESTIONS

1. Why is it so important to share the UDL Guidelines with your students?

2. Think back to your own schooling. Can you think of any hidden curriculum, or unintended messages, communicated to you or your classmates by your teachers?

3. Which Guidelines are most likely to get students involved in setting up your learning environment?

4. Which ideas outlined in this chapter will you implement right away? Can you think of any to add to the list?

# 5

# Next-Generation Skills in Today's Classrooms

In addition to aligning curriculum to rigorous standards, delivering that curriculum using universally designed methods, and empowering students to be expert learners, educators are also expected to help 21st-century students develop 21st-century skills.

Now, at this point, my mother, a rock star fifth-grade teacher who has been impacted by decades of education reform, would say something along the lines of, "Oh, great, now there is *another thing* we have to fit into our day. It's difficult enough to get through all the new standards, prepare for standardized testing, [insert all the other initiatives teachers balance on a daily basis . . .]" (Love you, Momma!) Here's the thing: she is

**Objective:** *You will learn how UDL allows you to incorporate important next-generation skills into your learning environment.*

**Rationale:** In order for our students to achieve their college, career, and life goals, they must be effective communicators, self-directed learners, creative problem-solvers, responsible citizens, and integrated thinkers. This may seem like yet another set of skills we have to add to our list of things to teach, but it doesn't have to be. When implementing UDL, you will be incorporating these skills and providing your students with a head start into a successful future.

100% correct. There is no time to do more, but there is a way to incorporate these skills into what you are already doing if you implement UDL. In fact, by implementing UDL, you are integrating critical cognitive and social skills.

In the book, *21st Century Skills: Learning for Our Times*, Trilling and Fadel (2009) refer to a recent study where 400 hiring executives of major corporations were asked if their new hires, recent college graduates, were prepared to work. Their answer, "not really," is a call for UDL to replace the model of traditional education, which did not prepare students for the careers of today. As a result, this "21st-century skills gap" is costing corporations an estimated $200 billion a year, worldwide, to educate an already educated workplace in important skills like critical thinking, teamwork, and work ethic (Trilling & Fadel, 2009).

We are well into the 21st century, and it's clear that these skills are not only important in today's classrooms but they are becoming more and more critical, and will be essential into the next century. They need a rebranding—and so we, as UDL practitioners, should start that movement. Enter, *next-generation skills!*

These next-generation skills need to be incorporated into our classrooms if we want our students to be successful. Research tells us that teachers play a significant role in helping students to develop these skills as they design and deliver education that integrates cognitive and social skills with content knowledge. Since we are preparing our students for the future, we must arm them with the knowledge and skills they need so they are ready to work and contribute to our global society.

Table 5-1 outlines the key domains for student success in the next generation: core subjects, learning and innovation skills, career and life skills, and the importance of productivity and accountability. Following, you will learn how a universally designed curriculum will provide opportunities for students to build these skills as they engage in your learning environment.

**TABLE 5-1:** Key Domains for Next-Generation Skills (Adapted from Trilling & Fadel [2009])

| KEY DOMAINS | ESSENTIAL NEXT-GENERATION SKILLS |
|---|---|
| Core subjects and skills | • Reading<br>• Writing<br>• Numeracy<br>• In other words, content needed to be an educated person |
| Learning and innovation skills | • Critical thinking<br>• Problem-solving<br>• Communications<br>• Creativity and innovation |
| Career and life skills | • Collaboration and teamwork<br>• Leadership and responsibility<br>• Initiative and self-direction<br>• Flexibility and adaptability<br>• Social and cross-cultural interaction<br>• Career and learning self-reliance |
| Productivity and accountability | • Digital literacy skills<br>• Computing literacy<br>• Information literacy<br>• ICT literacy<br>• Media literacy |

# CORE SUBJECTS AND SKILLS

In a universally designed classroom, teachers are learning experts, but that doesn't mean they don't need content expertise, as well. The expectation that teachers know their content has not changed—in fact,

I would argue that teachers' content knowledge is more important than ever before. In the traditional model of education, teachers were content experts, but how often were they questioned? How often were they challenged to explain their content in multiple ways? How often did they have to deliver the same content to many different audiences? Teachers today are the epitome of experts in their subject (oh, and they are also learning experts, which means they are superstars when delivering that content!).

The Danielson Framework, which has influenced educator evaluation in thousands of school systems worldwide, was revised in 2013 to clarify the importance of teacher content knowledge. Danielson explains:

> In order to guide student learning, teachers must have command of the subjects they teach. They must know which concepts and skills are central to a discipline and which are peripheral; they must know how the discipline has evolved into the 21st century, incorporating issues such as global awareness and cultural diversity. Accomplished teachers understand the internal relationships within the disciplines they teach, knowing which concepts and skills are prerequisite to the understanding of others. They are also aware of typical student misconceptions in the discipline and work to dispel them. But knowledge of the content is not sufficient; in advancing student understanding, teachers must be familiar with the particularly pedagogical approaches best suited to each discipline. (p. 7)

What is interesting about this definition of content knowledge is that there is an assumption that all teachers are expert learners who have the ability to model critical next-generation skills. In order to design and deliver your content, you have to be able to think critically to determine the most critical knowledge in your subject area, you have to communicate that information using methods that meet the needs of all learners, and you have to use creative and innovative practices (UDL!) to deliver that information. Congratulations! Being a successful teacher makes you a model of the importance of these next-generation skills.

# LEARNING AND INNOVATION SKILLS

> In most classrooms, students don't take an active role in their own learning, nor do they (respectfully) challenge the thinking of their classmates. All of this will represent a major departure, and therefore a major challenge, for many teachers.
>
> *(Danielson 2013, p. 3)*

As you remember, traditional education and differentiated instruction (DI) are both teacher-directed frameworks. In these models, students didn't have to learn *how* to learn because we served curriculum to them on a plate. In UDL, students take an active role in their learning so they can become expert learners.

When you provide students with challenging options to express their learning, they have to think critically about which options they will choose, use executive function skills to determine their strategy, incorporate important self-regulation skills to persist, and be creative about the outcomes of their assessment. By nature of giving students choices, they will have an opportunity to practice these skills. The "major challenge" identified by Danielson in the quote above is not something that will surface on your radar when you're implementing UDL.

Imagine, for example, that you want your students to read a piece of text and respond in some way to the text. In a traditional model of education, you, as a teacher, would select the text and ask students to read the text independently. After reading the text, students would respond to a predetermined question, using evidence from the text to support their answer. In elementary science, for example, students may read an article from *Scholastic News* about different animal families and respond to the question, "Which family has the most babies?" In high school anatomy and physiology, students may be required to read a section of their textbook on metabolism and nutrition. After reading the assigned text, you ask students to compare and contrast carbohydrate metabolism, lipid metabolism, and protein metabolism.

Tasks like those above certainly require content knowledge and reading comprehension skills, but they do not foster expert learning or innovation. Because these tasks do not require 21st-century skills, they do not prepare students for the world of work, where major corporations expect their hires to be self-directed, creative, and self-reliant.

If you were to universally design the lessons above, students would be required to use next-generation skills. When introducing animal families, for example, you could have various books about animals from the library, iPad apps cued to videos, images of animal families on a projected slide show, and stuffed animals around the room with name tags identifying the species. Students could explore these resources to build background knowledge before reading the article. For the assessment, students could work alone or in partners to create their product. Each student or group could select two animal families they learned about and explain how they are different by drawing two pictures, filling in a Venn diagram with words or pictures, writing a story about how they are different, or writing a note to the principal or a kindergarten teacher, explaining the differences. In this scenario, students have to create a goal for the resources they want to explore, select the assessment they want to complete, and think critically in order to create a response.

In the anatomy and physiology class, students could all use their devices to read articles about the different types of metabolism, explore videos, or meet in collaborative groups to build their understanding before reading the textbook. Instead of responding to the prompt, they could apply their knowledge in a more meaningful way. For example, you could provide students with hypothetical patients who have different dietary needs (i.e. the bodybuilder, the patient with hypothyroidism, the grandmother who needs to lose weight) and who have questions about their metabolism and how it will be affected by their new nutrition plan. Students could work in groups, as nutritionists, to create a resource for the patient to note how the diet would impact the different types of metabolism and how that would affect their overall system.

In both of these scenarios, students are reading and responding to text, but they are doing much more than that. Because they are immersed in a universally designed learning environment, they are solving problems, being creative, and working together.

# CAREER AND LIFE SKILLS

The UDL Guidelines provide us with strategies to build critical career and life skills in students. One of the Guidelines reminds us to provide options for students to collaborate with their peers to build engagement. When students collaborate on a group project, perform a skit together, complete a science lab with their peers, or play a game in class to review for a final exam, they are gaining valuable skills in teamwork. Like any skill, it's important to provide scaffolding to support teams of students. You can do this by teaching students the behaviors that are necessary to be an effective team player.

A study in the *American Journal of Business Education*, which examined which strategies are most effective at teaching teamwork in an MBA program, is widely applicable to teaching K–12 students. Hobson et al. (2014) began their article by stating, "Given the nearly universal use of workplace teams in U.S. businesses, perhaps no skill is more important for MBA students than facility with teamwork" (p. 191).

In their research, the authors created a tool (Table 5-2) to evaluate teamwork in these graduate students. They reviewed relevant literature on teamwork and created a list of positive behaviors and negative behaviors that contribute to a team's effectiveness. These lists are beneficial to use with your students, because they provide options for comprehension by highlighting patterns and critical features of highly functioning teams (and those behaviors that really need to be avoided). As with any new skill, it's important to provide graduated levels of support so students, regardless of age and variability, can practice these positive skills frequently, and receive mastery-oriented feedback throughout the process.

First, let's examine the list of behaviors that negatively affect team-building, so we can help our students (and maybe ourselves or our colleagues) learn to cope if they feel a tendency to showcase one of the skills below. Now, in full disclosure, when I first read this list in the research, I felt myself shrinking behind my computer, because I'm definitely guilty of side conversations from time to time. Now that I have completed this self-assessment, you can be sure that I have a new professional goal, which will include keeping my mouth shut until it's my turn to talk!

All joking aside, it's important to share this list with students so they are aware that these behaviors can prevent a team from being successful. The behaviors below limit a team's initiative and direction, impact the quality of the team's interactions, and affect the responsibility each individual has to the group. In short, these behaviors are barriers for students who need to build career and life skills.

Once your students know what *not* to do, it's important to highlight the skills that they need to successfully contribute to their group.

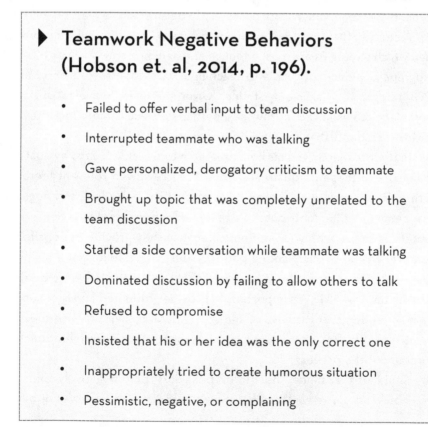

▶ **Teamwork Negative Behaviors (Hobson et. al, 2014, p. 196).**

- Failed to offer verbal input to team discussion

- Interrupted teammate who was talking

- Gave personalized, derogatory criticism to teammate

- Brought up topic that was completely unrelated to the team discussion

- Started a side conversation while teammate was talking

- Dominated discussion by failing to allow others to talk

- Refused to compromise

- Insisted that his or her idea was the only correct one

- Inappropriately tried to create humorous situation

- Pessimistic, negative, or complaining

**TABLE 5-2:** Teamwork Positive Behaviors (Adapted from Hobson et al., 2014, p. 196).

| BEHAVIOR | UDL CONSIDERATIONS |
|---|---|
| Listened attentively (eye contact, comprehends) when teammate was talking | Active listening increases comprehension and information-processing and minimizes distractions when teammates are sharing ideas. |
| Piggy-backed on teammate idea | Building on ideas fosters collaboration and community. |
| Gave positive feedback to teammate | Positive feedback promotes expectations and beliefs that optimize motivation. |
| Politely asked for input from a quiet teammate | Taking this initiative minimizes the threat and distraction of a nonparticipating teammate and helps to build community. |
| Offered task-related input during team discussion | This mastery-oriented feedback keeps the team engaged and moving forward. |
| Took notes on team discussion | Taking notes provides options for representation and will facilitate the team's ability to reflect. Also, a summary highlights patterns, critical features, big ideas, and relationships. |
| Attempted to achieve win-win resolutions to conflict | Building integrative thinking helps students to understand the importance of providing options to meet the needs of everyone on the team. |
| Kept team focused and "on-track" | Following a strategy strengthens the team's executive function. |
| Sought clarification by asking questions or paraphrasing | This allows team members to clarify ideas to heighten the salience of goals and objectives or big ideas. |
| Called teammates by their first name | Connecting on a personal level fosters collaboration and community. |
| Summarized areas of team agreement and disagreement | This work builds team self-assessment and reflection and also guides appropriate goal-setting for next steps. |
| Constructively criticized teammate ideas, not the person | This mastery-oriented feedback, when delivered in a culture that values feedback, can move a team forward. |

**TABLE 5-2:** Teamwork Positive Behaviors (Adapted from Hobson et al., 2014, p. 196) *CONTINUED*

| BEHAVIOR | UDL CONSIDERATIONS |
|---|---|
| Appropriately used humor to help team stay relaxed | This minimizes threats and provides an effective coping skill. |
| Answered teammate question | This collaboration is a coping strategy that builds collective knowledge. |
| Expressed empathy for teammate's feelings | This minimizes threats and provides an effective coping skill. |

The list of positive behaviors can be used in a variety of ways in your classroom. If you teach early elementary, you could write two books as a class—one about a good team and one about a naughty team. Discuss how they act toward one another. The class can illustrate the book. Elementary students could do the same or they can role-play and create skits about effective groups, and groups that are not effective. Before working in groups, they could review the list of positive behaviors and set personal goals of actions they want to practice during the group work. Middle school and high school students could have the list as a resource as they work in groups, and at various checkpoints the groups could reflect on the behaviors, discuss their overall effectiveness as a team, and set a group goal for the behaviors they want to focus on to improve their team's success. As with all things UDL, the options are endless.

After reviewing the lists of positive and negative behaviors, it's clear that becoming a team player is not an easy task. Since teamwork is a critical career and life skill, provide options for collaboration as often as possible, while highlighting the positive behaviors that allow teams to excel. This not only builds teamwork, but allows students to take initiative and responsibility for their behavior in a group.

One of the foundations of UDL is student-directed collaborative learning, which requires students to take roles in their teams, take collective initiative, set goals, and create strategies so they can be successful. This certainly won't happen overnight, but with enough opportunities to practice, students will build their executive function muscles and know that everything they need to be successful on a team is already inside them.

These career and life skills are not only crucial for students. They are important in our careers and lives. For a second, reflect how your team functions. It may be your grade-level team, department, or your amazing UDL PLC. If you dare, share the lists of behaviors at your next team meeting and facilitate a group self-assessment on your strengths. This is a great opportunity for you to flex your teamwork muscles, create goals and norms for future team collaborations, and have an awesome conversation about how to transfer these important skills to students.

# PRODUCTIVITY AND ACCOUNTABILITY

To be productive in today's world, one must utilize technology to develop digital, computing, information, and media literacy. There are countless tools at students' fingerprints that can increase their efficiency and productivity if they know how to use them, but like any form of literacy, these skills need to be scaffolded.

The National Education Technology Plan (2016), titled "Future Ready Learning," emphasizes the importance of Universal Design for Learning as a means of personalizing learning and as a framework for designing and deploying educational technologies in effective, meaningful ways." As a UDL practitioner, you can foster digital and media literacy in all three UDL principles. To increase engagement and help students to sustain effort and persistence, there are numerous digital tools where students can collaborate in the cloud. McKee-Waddell (2015) identifies a list of collaborative writing tools that students can use when working toward standards together (Table 5-3). Encourage collaborative groups to explore some of the tools and then allow them to use the tool that is the most accessible to them—the process can build teamwork, as well.

**TABLE 5-3:** Resources to Improve and Enhance Digital Writing: Collaborative Writing Tools (Adapted from McKee-Waddell, 2015, p. 25).

| TOOL | DESCRIPTION |
|---|---|
| TitanPad | Allows students to work on one document simultaneously |
| Google Docs | Allows students to collaborate on a writing project, spreadsheets, or presentations |
| StackEdit | Allows students to synchronize, publish, and share documents |
| PBworks | Host and share information; classroom subscription required |
| Typewrite | Allows real-time editing, syncs with Dropbox, and enables easy sharing and editing of different versions |
| Quip | Edit, discuss, and share in one place |
| Penflip | Helps students write better with others |
| Hackpad | Simple to use, real-time wiki with innovative features; a collaborative editing tool similar to Google Docs |

Providing students with digital devices and options to explore content using multiple means of representation gives them practice with digital and media literacy, as well. Just as it's important to read books to develop early literacy, it is also important to study texts such as blogs, videos, and apps to become familiar with the structure and purpose of the tools. When you provide students with choices to build their background knowledge, learn new vocabulary, and build comprehension in what used to be a traditional lecture, they become engaged and self-directed, which allows you to be more efficient and productive when monitoring their progress and providing mastery-oriented feedback. It's a win-win of next-generation skill-building.

Lastly, providing options for students to use these technologies to express their skills and knowledge of content in authentic tasks creates an environment where they are encouraged to build digital literacy across the content area. Paper and pencil, near obsolete, do not have the same potential.

Hopefully now you see that by implementing UDL, you're also teaching these next-generation skills that are critical for student success—and for your success, as well. We aren't born experts at these skills; we learn them along the way. Still learning the tools? That's even better! You can model the characteristics of an expert learner as you work alongside technology integration specialists to catapult today's classroom into the next generation.

# SUMMARY

All next-generation skills find their place in the UDL Guidelines. When you universally design your curriculum, you provide options so students have an opportunity to collaborate, build executive function and self-regulation skills, and experiment with multiple tools to communicate and build literacy. This is how students build these critical next-generation skills.

# DISCUSSION QUESTIONS

1. Review all the next-generation skills. Which skills are your strengths and which skills do you still want to strengthen? How can UDL help you to build those skills?

2. Which skills are the ones that are most lacking in your students? If your students never build those skills, how will that affect their future?

3. After reviewing the list of positive teamwork behaviors, how would you assess your students' ability to work as a team?

4. Prepare an elevator speech: How does UDL help students build critical next-generation skills?

# Two Types of Learning Standards and UDL Implementation

**6**

One possible criticism of UDL is that it focuses too much on engaging students and not enough on academic rigor and learning. This could not be further from the truth. UDL is a rigorous curriculum-design process that begins with standards-based alignment. All teachers have content standards we are required to meet. To be successful, students need to master those standards. To ensure that students do this, it's necessary to design the curriculum with the standards in mind. And, of course, we start with the *why* to heighten the salience of goals and objectives as we build engagement in our students.

Now, you may be thinking that your standards are too difficult for your students, but you have to work to change

**Objective:** *You will understand the two different types of curriculum standards and how each type lends itself to different UDL strategies.*

**Rationale:** In this chapter, I want to encourage you to examine your teaching standards to determine which standards encourage choice and which have the means embedded and require scaffolding. This will make it easier to design your UDL lessons.

that mind-set. Learning from a grade-level appropriate curriculum is not a privilege. It's a right for all students. Whether they seem prepared is irrelevant. It's our job as teachers to fill in the gaps for students so they can have a challenging course of study with academic rigor.

The Integrated Comprehensive Systems for Equity (ICS) is a systems approach to eliminate inequities for all students. The system is built on a foundation of four equity non-negotiables: focus on equity, align staff and students, transform teaching and learning, and leverage policy and funding (Frattura & Capper, 2016).

Often, when school districts prepare to implement UDL, they focus on transforming teaching and learning, but without other structures and supports in place, a true transformation for all students will not occur. ICS provides us with a step-by-step model that ensures that our schools and systems are capable of supporting and scaling up best practices like UDL. The first cornerstone reminds us, "Changing the system to eliminate inequities begins with ourselves. The system is responsible for the prevention of student failure." Think about the power of that statement. If we want all of our students to succeed, we must believe that we are capable of providing every student, regardless of variability, with a rigorous, standards-based, universally designed education. If we fail to build the foundation of this first cornerstone, many of our students will never get to access the education they deserve. Now, a belief in equity is not a panacea, but it's a start. You need to focus on equity and hold high expectations for all students before you can begin to transform teaching and learning.

An interesting study in urban middle schools in greater Philadelphia looked at the importance of teaching grade-level standards to students who are struggling. Researchers studied the differences between high-performing schools and low-performing schools and discovered a key difference in how the different types of schools responded to standards (Brown, Anfara, & Roney, 2004). In response to the question, "Do you teach a standards-based curriculum in this school?" and "How do you feel about doing this?" teachers from the high-performing schools answered that the standards supported what they already did in their classrooms. In contrast, teachers at the low-performing schools reported that the standards were imposed on them by a system that did not take into account students' abilities (or lack thereof). These schools had similar student populations. The study showed that high-performing schools had curriculum aligned to the standards and teachers who believed that all students could be successful. These teachers focused on equity. This message was undoubtedly communicated to students in the curriculum.

If you don't believe your students will achieve standards, there's a good chance they won't, because your beliefs become a self-fulfilling prophecy, or the phenomenon where the inaccurate belief that something will happen will actually cause it to occur (Merton, 1948). In theory, this phenomenon can happen in the classroom. That's a scary thought.

To avoid negative self-fulfilling prophecies, it's important to align your curriculum with grade-level standards and then fix your curriculum so students can achieve those standards. It's not within the scope of our job to predict how a student will do in the future. It's our job to teach standards-based content to every student, exactly where they are.

At this point, you have a basic understanding of the UDL Guidelines and some options to recruit students into your learning environment, and the importance of incorporating next generation skills into your practice. You also know that you need to teach grade-level standards to students who may not be able to access them on their own. Now, you may be wondering how to actually plan rigorous lessons to help your students meet the standards. Where do you start? There is one simple change of practice that you can begin right away that will set the ball rolling.

One of the most powerful strategies is to become familiar with your state's standards in your subject area and post a standard of focus on the board each day. Responsiveness to standards is important, because standards ensure that students receive a rigorous, balanced education. Your state's standards include all content and skills that students will need to be successful in the world as adults, so it's so important that educators fully understand what the standards are so we can help students to meet them.

That is why it is so important to commit to your standards and post them on the board each day. It may seem boring, but it doesn't have to be. I once observed a class where the teacher gave his standards superhero powers, and the kids loved it. This teacher's agenda board identified the "Superhero Standards" for the day. The state standard was Batman's standard of the day while the objective was attributed to Superman. The agenda board was decorated with large posters of the superheroes. On the day of the observation, Batman's standard of the day was, "Batarands are not my greatest asset in battle. Standard 14.4 is," and then Standard 14.4 was listed. Superman's objective for the day was, "My body is enhanced by the earth's yellow sun to analyze the effects of sound and figurative language."

Talk about engaging students! If we all posted our standards on the board every day, our students would know what was expected of them, and they could appreciate that the curriculum is not just an end in itself. Also, the standards would serve as a reminder to us that there should be an objective to the lesson. Just posting the standards is a step in the right direction because all of a sudden, you become aware of the messages you're sending to students about the curriculum and you'll also see if your curriculum is aligned to the standards. Also, you can prove to students (and parents and administrators) that you did your job if they try to give you any flak about it.

Posting standards on the board and requiring students to study a challenging curriculum is obviously not a panacea. Without effective instruction and engaging activities, challenging material may not be accessible for students. Teachers need effective strategies to help all students respond to the challenge of rigorous curriculum, and this is where UDL comes in, and this is what takes time.

Since UDL is a standards-based curriculum design, however, we have to start with the standards. If possible, take out your standards and have them in front of you, because this process is easier if your standards are accessible. As you read your standards, you'll notice that some standards require students to have specific knowledge, while others require them to complete specific tasks. This is the difference between content standards and methods standards, or standards with specific tasks, or *means*, embedded. The difference between the two types of standards needs to be understood because each type of standard lends itself to different UDL strategies.

# REVIEW OF THE TWO TYPES OF STANDARDS

Content standards identify concepts that students have to know, while methods standards note tasks that students have to complete. As teachers, we know that many of the tasks have to be completed by following specific steps, such as writing an essay, solving an algebraic equation, completing a science lab using the inquiry method, or serving a volleyball. By looking at just the first verb in a standard, you can often identify whether the student will have to learn a concept or perform a skill. Note the difference between the following verbs:

| CONTENT STANDARDS ASK STUDENTS TO... | METHODS STANDARDS ASK STUDENTS TO... |
|---|---|
| Describe | Perform |
| Explain | Create |
| Analyze | Write |
| Summarize | Sing |
| Identify | Use |
| Give examples | Demonstrate |
| Discuss | Solve |
| Differentiate | |
| Compare and contrast | |
| Learn | |

As you can see, content standards require students to internalize information. Since you can't directly assess what is in a student's brain, they must express knowledge explicitly. Instead of always assessing this knowledge in an essay or a multiple-choice test, you have an opportunity to allow them to present their understanding in an engaging way.

Methods standards, on the other hand, have a definite end product in mind. Because you can't be so flexible with the task, you have to provide options for scaffolding so all students will be able to complete the task with proficiency. More on how to do this in Chapter 8.

Tables 6-1 and 6-2 include examples of each type of standard for major subject areas in elementary and secondary grades. Standards are from the Massachusetts Curriculum Frameworks.

**TABLE 6-1:** Content vs. Methods Standards, Elementary

| | CONTENT STANDARD | METHODS STANDARD |
|---|---|---|
| Art | Learn and use appropriate vocabulary related to methods, materials, and techniques. | Create 2D and 3D artwork from direct observation. *For example, students draw a still life of flowers or fruit, action studies of their classmates in sports poses, or sketches of the class pet having a snack or a nap.* |
| English/ language arts/reading | Describe characters, settings, and major events in a story, using key details. | Write opinion pieces on topics or texts, supporting a point of view with reasons. |
| Math | Explain why addition and subtraction strategies work, using place value and the properties of operations. | Count to 100 by ones and by tens. |
| Music | Perceive, describe, and respond to basic elements of music, including beat, tempo, rhythm, meter, pitch, melody, texture, dynamics, harmony, and form. | Sing independently, maintaining accurate intonation, steady tempo, rhythmic accuracy, appropriately produced sound (timbre), clear diction, and correct posture. |
| Physical education | Identify physical and psychological changes that result from participation in a variety of physical activities. | Perform rhythm routines, including dancing, to demonstrate fundamental movement skills. |
| Science | Give examples of how the surface of the earth changes due to slow processes such as erosion and weathering, and rapid processes such as landslides, volcanic eruptions, and earthquakes. | Read, interpret, and analyze a combination of ground-based observations, satellite data, and computer models to demonstrate Earth systems and their interconnections. |
| Social studies | Explain the meaning of the stars and stripes in the American flag, and describe official procedures for the care and display of the flag. | Use map and globe skills to determine absolute locations (latitude and longitude) of places studied. |

**TABLE 6-2:** Content vs. Methods Standards, Secondary

|  | CONTENT STANDARD | METHODS STANDARD |
|---|---|---|
| Art | Demonstrate the ability to describe the kinds of imagery used to represent subject matter and ideas, for example, literal representation, simplification, abstraction, or symbolism. | Create artwork that shows knowledge of the ways in which architects, craftsmen, and designers develop abstract symbols by simplifying elements of the environment. |
| English/ language arts/reading | Explain the function of phrases and clauses in general and their function in specific sentences. | Write arguments to support claims in an analysis of substantive topics or texts, using valid reasoning and relevant and sufficient evidence. |
| Math | Describe events as subsets of a sample space (the set of outcomes) using characteristics (or categories) of the outcomes, or as unions, intersections, or complements of other events ("or," "and," "not"). | Derive the formula $A = 1/2\ ab\ \sin(C)$ for the area of a triangle by drawing an auxiliary line from a vertex perpendicular to the opposite side. |
| Music | Compare and contrast ways in which compositional devices and techniques are used in two or more examples of the same piece, genre, or style. | Perform with expression and technical accuracy a large repertoire of solo and ensemble literature representing various genres, styles, and cultural and historical periods, with a level of difficulty of 4, on a scale of 1 to 6. |
| Physical education | Identify the components of physical fitness and the factors involved in planning and evaluating fitness programs for individuals at different stages of the life cycle. | Demonstrate developmentally appropriate competence (basic skills, strategies, and rules) in many and proficiency in a few movement forms and motor skills (team sports, aquatics, individual/dual sports, outdoor pursuits, self-defense, dance, and gymnastics). |

**TABLE 6-2:** Content vs. Methods Standards, Secondary *CONTINUED*

|  | CONTENT STANDARD | METHODS STANDARD |
|---|---|---|
| Science | Identify and describe three subsystems of a transportation vehicle or device, i.e., structural, propulsion, guidance, suspension, control, and support. | Properly use instruments, equipment, and materials (e.g., scales, probeware, meter sticks, microscopes, computers) including setup, calibration (if required), technique, maintenance, and storage. |
| Social studies/ history | Describe the rise and goals of totalitarianism in Italy, Germany, and the Soviet Union, and analyze the policies and ideas of Mussolini, Hitler, Lenin, and Stalin. | Formulate a savings or financial investment plan for a future goal (e.g., college or retirement). |

## ▶ Practice: PLC Assignment #1

**Objective:** *When examining your standards, try to identify whether each standard is a content standard or a methods standard. If it is a content standard,* students can be very creative about how they express their knowledge. On the other hand, if a standard states how students will demonstrate their knowledge, you'll need to provide supports and scaffolds for students who may struggle with achieving the standard independently. All students should be given options to access the scaffolds, as they may be helpful to students you wouldn't expect.

**Rationale:** In order to design and implement UDL in the classroom, it's important to understand exactly what you are responsible for teaching. Analyzing standards and categorizing the content of those standards as knowledge or skills is imperative to determine which UDL Guidelines are most applicable when designing and delivering learning experiences.

## Your Turn

Step 1: Choose a set of standards to analyze. Options:

- Choose one subject, one level, or one unit you teach and examine those standards.

- The number of standards will vary based on the subject. If you're looking for a number, try to examine at least five standards, although you may examine many more.

Step 2: Determine your audience. Your audience will impact the format, the level of detail, and the transferability of this project. Options:

- Your students or learners

- Parents or the community

- Colleagues

- Self

Step 3: Determine which aspects of the standards require students to *know*, and which require learners to *do*. Options:

- Create a table with two or more columns, an artistic representation, or some other model to differentiate between the knowledge and the skills.

- You may choose to add an additional column of prerequisite skills that learners would need before learning the new knowledge outlined in the standard.

- If the standards are predominantly knowledge standards, note the application of that knowledge (i.e., what are some ways that students can apply or practice that knowledge).

- If the standards are predominantly skill-based, view previous standards in the vertical alignment to determine what background knowledge is inherent in the skill.

# Content Standards and UDL Strategies

Now that you have your standards separated, it's time to start focusing on the UDL Educator Guidelines that best serve each type of standard. To review, a content standard outlines information that students need to learn and understand. The standard does not tell you exactly how students need to express that knowledge, so there is a great opportunity to give students choice. For example, by the end of Grade 3, students must know from memory all products of two one-digit numbers.

Standards do not note how this information needs to be learned or expressed. Students could learn products in countless ways—memorizing the numbers on a chart, using manipulatives like crayons or macaroni, playing flashcard games with friends, and so on. Similarly, students could express their knowledge in countless ways. They could tell you orally, speak on video or audio recorder, write the products, take a traditional quiz, and so forth.

Students love choice. Children and adolescents have little control over their lives, so they will take it wherever they can get it. Even the perceived element of choice seems to increase student buy-in. When giving students choice, you are still in control since you are presenting them with acceptable choices. The important thing is to ensure that all choices allow students to model proficiency on the chosen standard. When you design assessments with your standards in mind using the UDL lesson planning process, you can be sure that regardless of what they choose, they will have the opportunity to model proficiency while incorporating next-generation skills.

One common criticism of giving students choices is that students will choose the same activities for every assignment. You may have one student who loves flashcards, so whenever he needs to remember new content, he chooses that method. That is not a problem. If the child demonstrates proficiency with the chosen standard, that child is learning. He feels confident and has learned a strategy that works for him. Eventually, he will probably tire of the flashcard strategy and choose another; as his teacher, you could certainly encourage him to choose other options. That's the great thing about UDL. It's a flexible way of teaching. Chapter 7 presents templates for choice assignments and outlines a number of choices that may interest students.

# Methods Standards and UDL Strategies

The next type of standard is the methods standard, also known as a standard with the means, or the skills, embedded. There are some standards that note exactly what a student must be able to do. In math, students must solve equations using certain formulas; in English, students have to write narratives; in physical education, students must take physical fitness tests; in science, students must follow specific multi-step procedures. Students don't have a choice, and the UDL framework makes allowances for this fact. When students have to master a specific skill, there are UDL guidelines that encourage teachers to provide options for students to activate their background knowledge, provide models and rubrics, and provide mastery-oriented feedback. Together, these practices provide invaluable scaffolding for students.

The original theory of scaffolded instruction grew from Vygotsky's research (1978) on the zone of proximal development (ZPD), the distance between a learner's actual developmental level and her potential developmental level as determined by the guidance of a more knowledgeable individual (you!). Put simply, it's the difference between what a student can accomplish alone and what that same student can accomplish with the support of an effective teacher.

Our students come to us with vast variability. They have unique experiences, background knowledge, intellectual skills, and physical abilities that make them different from each other. Regardless of their differences, we need all of them to meet minimum proficiency levels while performing specific tasks. Meeting or exceeding our standards is the level we want all our students to be at, so we need to design curriculum to help bridge the gap between where students are and where they need to be.

Many people who hear about UDL for the first time say things like, "Oh, that sounds a lot like differentiated instruction (DI)." But as you learned in an earlier chapter, it's not. In a DI curriculum, a teacher creates lessons and assessments with various levels of challenge and distributes them to students, based on their perceived level of ability. For example, many textbooks include activities for struggling readers, advanced learners, and struggling writers. In theory, if teachers implemented this DI curriculum, some students would have access to challenging curriculum, while others are given a modified, or negotiated, curriculum. In short, students are labeled, and there are no labels in UDL. There are only fabulous, amazing students with different levels of variability.

With this in mind, you can design curriculum with rich scaffolding so that no student feels embarrassed to complete the work. As far as we've come in society, students still feel the stigma of a special education title, but UDL eliminates that feeling of being seen as "less-than." When you design your lessons using scaffolds for every potential student you could ever have, you help all students meet their highest potential. If students don't need the scaffolds, they simply won't use them, but as long as they are there, you won't need to accommodate the lesson for other students.

We've already established that scaffolding is an important skill for UDL educators. It's also important for diverse learners when it embodies four key features: active engagement, intersubjectivity, ongoing diagnosis, and transfer of responsibility (Puntambekar & Hübscher, 2005). All four features relate directly to UDL.

*Active engagement* refers not only to students but to teachers, as well. In order for students to succeed, teachers and students need to be actively engaged in designing and delivering curriculum, presenting lessons, and providing valuable feedback, while students work on expressing their knowledge. This is a huge shift in education. If you watch any movie from the 1950s with a classroom scene, you'll see students sitting silently in rows of desks while a teacher sips coffee and corrects papers. Although that would be nice, it doesn't help students to achieve their fullest potential. You as a teacher need to be engaged, as well.

*Intersubjectivity* is an important feature because it clarifies the important relationship between you as a teacher and your students. When you think about that relationship, it's sometimes goosebump-worthy. Here's why. Your students need you to construct knowledge—not someone down the hall, not their parents, but you. Your students build knowledge because you, as a more knowledgeable individual, provide options for all students to access content and skills in an engaging way that helps them to learn. You know your students better than anyone, so use scaffolding techniques that are helpful and relevant to them. A 1st-grade teacher needs to provide much different scaffolds than a college professor, but they have something in common. Both teachers examine the learning task and their students and design hints, tips, and everyday wisdom to push students from the level where they are to the highest level they can achieve. That's exciting stuff.

*Ongoing diagnosis* allows you to increase the volume of mastery-oriented feedback. Building scaffolds into the curriculum design process frees up a lot of time to provide that rich, meaningful feedback that students need. Often, much class time is spent answering students' questions about the format of assignments. If you provide exemplars, rubrics, and checklists, and allow students to work collaboratively, you have eliminated countless questions and you can spend class time helping students improve and deepen their understanding of topics instead of answering "How long does this need to be?" 15 times.

*Transfer of responsibility* is key because ultimately students must complete work independently. This release of responsibility allows students to build fluencies with graduated levels of support for practice and performance. Some practitioners hear about UDL, note its focus on collaborative work, and then write it off, saying, "Well, every student has to take his or her own test at the end of the year, so I'm not assigning group work all the time." The collaboration is just a point on the continuum before students can complete their own work and a necessary skill for next-generation success.

As students move away from teacher-directed learning and begin to self-direct their own learning, they begin to internalize learning concepts. Working with peers helps to further internalize this knowledge. To transfer responsibility to students, the first step is for you to model the skills that students are expected to master and explain explicitly what you are doing, providing work exemplars if necessary. After modeling, students can practice the skills in collaborative groups. The final step is for students to work individually to accomplish necessary learning tasks.

To recap, scaffolding is not just about handing out a rubric and allowing students to work in groups. It's about being engaged with students as they construct knowledge, working with them to bridge the gap between where they are and where they can be, providing feedback throughout a lesson, and transferring responsibility to them so they can complete work independently.

Before getting into how you can scaffold instruction for students, let's take a look at an example of exceptional scaffolding that occurred in a college science course. It's a great example because it drives home the point that scaffolding is not just for struggling students. Effective scaffolded instruction brings all learners to higher levels of achievement.

Li-hsuan Yang, an assistant professor of integrated science at the University of Michigan, provided scaffolding to students because they were struggling with applying their understanding of light and vision to real-world situations. Yang (2009) began the lesson by challenging students to answer three questions about how distance affects how they see themselves in a mirror. Students then tested their predictions, which allowed them to recognize misconceptions, while Yang diagnosed specific problem areas. One common misconception was "the mirror captures half of its surroundings no matter where you stand." To address this error, Yang provided a sketch of a top-down view of the classroom to explain that the farther away a person is from a mirror, the narrower the background becomes in the reflection. While students continued to empirically test the questions, Yang probed their techniques, leading them to accurate conclusions. At the completion of the lesson, students could contribute to a more useful discussion about light and vision.

Yang's lesson was effective because it embodied the features of successful scaffolding. Students were actively engaged and constructed their own knowledge. They were encouraged to make predictions, test their ideas, and collaborate with their teacher. With Yang close by, problems were identified and addressed accordingly. Finally, responsibility was released to students so they could accurately discuss the concepts of light and vision unaided.

Yang's class includes one example of a scaffolded lesson. There are many additional scaffolding examples in Chapter 8, including templates for creating student assignments.

# SUMMARY

If you examine your standards closely, you will notice that some focus on students acquiring knowledge, while others focus on students acquiring specific skills. To get the most out of your UDL practice, it's important to determine how to align standards to the different UDL Guidelines as you plan your lessons.

# DISCUSSION QUESTIONS

1. If you were asked "Do you teach a standards-based curriculum in this school?" and "How do you feel about doing this?" what would your answer be and why?

2. When examining your standards, do you have more content standards or methods standards? Does that change the way you view your curriculum-design process?

3. Are you more comfortable providing students with choice or scaffolded instruction? Why?

4. At this point, what are your thoughts about UDL?

# 7

# Choice Assignments
## *Expressing Knowledge in Endless Ways*

Everyone reading this has probably been to a wedding. If you're anything like me, you start to get excited when you receive an official invitation with the meal-selection card. That's practically my favorite part of the whole wedding experience. I love looking at the small, white embossed card and checking off my dinner selection. I always choose the fish!

You love choice. When you attend a wedding or go to a restaurant, you expect to have choices. If you're a vegetarian, you do not want to be staring at a big slab of prime rib. On the other hand, if you're the meat-and-potatoes type, the thought of a tofu kebab may not be so appetizing. Most brides and grooms understand that their guests are different and their

**Objective:** *You will be able to develop choice assignments to assess student understanding of your content standards.*

**Rationale:** There is nothing more important than giving students choice. This chapter contains content-specific lessons for the core subjects and content-neutral templates for choice assignments and then provides 20 creative ideas, or choices, to put in the assignments.

diets have much variability. That is why most weddings have a choice of food, a buffet, or passed appetizers. These different choices allow everyone to fill their bellies with food they love.

This is true in countless other settings, as well. When you're shopping at the grocery store, there are 20 brands of peanut butter; if you're ever gone to the nail salon, you've probably spent 10 minutes mulling over minute differences in shades of red. We buy our iPhone cases in different colors, for goodness sake! As adults, we expect choice, and when we don't have the liberty to make a choice (jury duty, anyone?), we feel stifled, controlled, and frustrated. Imagine that feeling and bottle it. That's how students feel when we don't provide choice for them.

When we hand out assignments, students want choice as much as we do as adults. Don't serve the proverbial prime rib if it's not necessary. You owe it to students to help them practice making choices. (If you have an indecisive friend, you know how important this skill is in adulthood. "I don't care where we go; where do you want to go?") Once you have separated your standards into content standards and methods standards, you're ready to start designing your UDL lessons. First, we'll focus on the choice assignment, which is an assessment where students can choose how to express their knowledge to you.

Most teachers find that choice assignments are the most fun to plan because they require the most student creativity and often student work will blow your mind. I've heard countless times, "I can't believe the students put so much time and effort into this. It was just a homework assignment." The thing is that students want to be engaged, but they need to be excited to learn. When they have choice, they feel empowered and they want to own their assignment.

Providing students with options to express their learning allows them to build career and life skills and learning and innovative skills. First, students must take the initiative and set a goal for their assessment by selecting the option that works best for them. As a next step, they have an opportunity to build executive function as they create their strategy and determine which materials they will need to be successful. The options also allow students to be creative, collaborate with peers, and communicate in innovative ways.

Choice assignments really tap into student engagement. The UDL Guidelines remind teachers to provide options for recruiting interest and note the importance of optimizing individual choice and autonomy. This increases the value of the assignment. Lastly, students need to feel comfortable choosing the option that is most engaging to them. If a student loves to sing, for example, he or she needs to know that students will not laugh or make fun of the performance. Setting up a class culture where students respect each other allows students to take risks. Embarrassing yourself doesn't hurt either. If you're willing to go up in front of the class and sing a rap about photosynthesis, other students will probably follow your lead.

Before reviewing a sample assignment template, let's start by examining a number of creative ideas that students could choose, regardless of grade level or ability. You can adapt these ideas to your own class and also add ideas once you talk to your students. All of these activities allow students to express their understanding of concepts without using traditional methods. Use them in place of your traditional assessments and see how your students react.

## TWENTY FABULOUS IDEAS FOR CHOICE ASSIGNMENTS

### 1

Have students tweet their understanding of a concept using 140 characters or less. You may need them to tutor you on their short-hand acronyms. This is a great assignment for students who actually tweet, but it's also a fun learning opportunity for younger students who are learning to count. You can teach them what a character is and then ask them to count each character as they write an answer. You can challenge students to see who can get the closest to 140 characters without going over. Tweeting is especially a great activity for identifying the main idea or concept or when providing an objective summary of a piece of text.

Some schools have even have Twitter unblocked for students to use during the day. If this is true at your school, students could log on and tweet answers to questions using specific hashtags. You could have an intellectual class discussion without using words. The possibilities with Twitter are really endless. Here is one example of how I used Twitter at the beginning of the year:

Activator: Your objective is to write me a tweet that is 140 characters or less, introducing yourself and sharing some information that will help me to get to know you a bit better.

## 2

You could also ask students to create a Facebook or Instagram page to outline their understanding of a topic. You can have them include status updates, pictures, comments, likes, and so on. Many students are so tech savvy that they will create a very realistic Facebook page. Students can add real pictures to their page or can draw pictures of concepts, diagrams, and so forth. They can create the page as themselves or a literary or historical character. An inanimate object could even have a Facebook page. For example, a nucleus could have a pretty cool page. If your students aren't familiar with Facebook, you could show them a public page of a respectable celebrity or political figure. Also, many education think-tanks, as well as famous authors, now have Facebook pages. If you want to provide students with a Facebook template, there are countless ones online.

## 3

Artistic students will love to create graphic novels or comic strips examining content under study. Political cartoons can be used as exemplars with older students since they communicate complex concepts in simple drawings. If the whole class is interested, you could make a book of the cartoons, or you could take pictures and make an e-book that you could post on your class webpage. Students love to see their work published. If students save each page as a PDF, they can even turn it into an online book using Flipsnack, a site that allows users to convert photos and PDF files into online magazines, or flipbooks, for free.

**4**

Some students love to design, write, and illustrate children's books about complex topics. Although a children's book may seem elementary for older students, asking them to assess their audience and explain a process in simple terms requires higher-order thinking and a true understanding of the topic. One way to make this extra engaging is to contact elementary-school teachers in the district and ask if they would like to read the books to their classes. Better yet, maybe your students can take a field trip and read the books to the students, or you could make a video recording of them reading the text. Students can write books on anything from nuclear fusion to volcanic eruption to healthy eating, like the fabulous text shown in Figure 7-1, *Billy Broccoli and the Fruit Garden* written by my former middle school students.

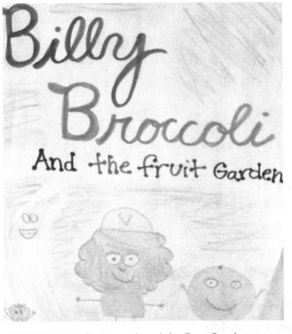

**FIGURE 7-1:** *Billy Broccoli and the Fruit Garden*

## 5

Writing poetry does not have to be an assignment only from English teachers. Teachers across the content area can give students the option of writing poetry to express their understanding of concepts. Imagine a Shakespearean sonnet about acceleration in a physics class. Allow humanities and the sciences to collide. You could also have students write a poem in a voice not their own. Students might choose to write in the voice of some historical figure, in the voice of a scientist, in the voice of someone they know, or in the voice of a character from a story or movie. Even young students could write a haiku and get extra practice in counting syllables.

## 6

Some students still love the traditional poster. Put out a variety of materials like crayons, markers, colored pencils, glitter, glue, and construction paper. Even college students begin to get excited about the prospect of incorporating glitter into a project. Stickers and stamps are big hits, too. They bring out the child in everyone.

## 7

If the poster idea sounds too messy, a variety of sites allow you to create posters or multimedia presentations online. You can require students to use a combination of words and images to show their understanding of a topic by encouraging them to use one of the following sites:

- Animoto (www.animoto.com): Students can create professional looking video slideshows accompanied by music.

- Powtoon (www.powtoon.com): Students can create animated videos and presentations using the same site that 8 million customers use worldwide—including many Fortune 500 companies.

- Smore (www.smore.com): Students can create a professional-looking electronic newsletter.

- Voki (www.voki.com): Students can create a talking avatar to present information on their behalf.

## 8

While many teachers encourage students to create PowerPoints to show their understanding of concepts, I recommend using Prezi.com, which takes PowerPoint to the next level. Instead of slides, there is one canvas, and users move around the canvas, zooming in on important content. Signing up is free and students can access their presentations from home.

## 9

Some students love to put on a show (you know the ones!). A pretend talk show is a fun way to do this. Students can create a talk-show script, interviewing an important figure in your curriculum. Encourage students to show up in costume and act it out or record it at home and bring it in. If young students aren't familiar with the talk-show format, you can show them an episode of *Ellen*. She interviews kids often, so there would be episodes you could show even the youngest students.

## 10

Similar to the talk show, you could invite students to "be the character" from a book or an important figure and come to class in character, with costume and accents, and all other classmates can ask questions. This requires great preparation, but I am sure you have some kids who would love to rise to that challenge and the rest of the class would remember it forever. I still remember "Noah Webster" came into my class in graduate school, and when asked of his greatest achievement, he answered, "Changing words like *colour* to *color*." Every time I open a dictionary, I laugh.

# 11

In almost any class, students can create a board game to express their knowledge of content. Challenge students to create a game, write the rules of the game, and then demonstrate how to play. As a review for the test, you could actually play the game with the class. This is especially great with older students who thrive on competition.

# 12

Have students complete a Role-Audience-Form-Topic (RAFT) prompt. Within a RAFT, students make choices about who they are as a writer, who their audience is, which format they want to use, and, finally, what topic they want to write about. Either you can provide students with rows, where the role and audience match the task, like the following table, or you can allow students to mix and match to create hundreds of possible prompts.

| ROLE | AUDIENCE | FORM | TOPIC |
|------|----------|------|-------|
| Politician running for office | General public | Public service commercial | Argue your position on an environmental issue on your list. |
| King Earth | Loyal subjects | Proclamation | Argue that all subjects should spread the word about recycling. |
| Graniteville Road | Department of Public Works | Interview | Inform the DPW, in an interview script, that you can't be salted. |
| Cape Cod Sound | Congress | Illustrated poem | Narrate your day when the wind turbines were constructed. |

The *role* of the writer in a RAFT is the person who students become when they are writing. Students adopt a first-person voice and write as someone else. They could be a famous writer, like Mark Twain; a mathematician, like Euclid; a native of Ghana; even a nucleus. Regardless of the content, students can adopt a viewpoint different from their own. The role can be historical, fictional, animate, inanimate, futuristic, or even magical.

The *audience* is who they are writing to. Are they writing informally to a friend? Writing formally to a person of importance? Are they writing to one individual or a group of people? Students must think about their intended audience when drafting their response.

The *format* is the genre of writing. Will students write a letter? A public service announcement? Could they create a Facebook page? A poem? A public speech?

Lastly, students need to consider the *task*. In a traditional RAFT, the *T* stands for topic + strong verb, which really means, what's the writing task? Why are they writing? Not only do they need to choose a purpose for writing, but they need to take it a step further and consider why they are writing. Are they writing to persuade someone to take a certain course of action, or do they simply want to inform an audience about a new opportunity?

There are many sample RAFTs online if you search for them. If you do, you'll see that the possibilities are indeed endless and you can adapt the assignment for any grade and content area. Given that there are so many choices for students, using RAFTs as a strategy is a great way to engage students.

## 13

One of my former colleagues asked students to complete a Dinner Party prompt, where they write a skit, imagining a group of characters are out to a fine dinner. What would they order? What would they say to one another? This prompt could be done with scientists, historical figures, and so forth. You could provide students with a list of possible attendees or have them invite additional guests, which they learn about through enrichment work or independent study.

## 14

Ask students to write a business letter to someone regarding the content under study. For example, if you teach economics, you could ask students to write a business letter to the owner of their fictional rent-controlled apartment, regarding the principles of supply and demand. In science, students could write a letter to a racecar driver, explaining how acceleration is not only moving forward but also moving backward and turning.

# 15

Even more valuable than a business letter may be a business e-mail. Many students (and sometimes adults!) write e-mails too informally, and it's good practice to learn how to draft one in a formal tone. Provide students with the following tips if they choose this assignment:

**Subject** The subject line should contain an informative, detailed subject so the reader can decide whether to read the message or delete it. Don't say something like "Important" because the content may not be important to the reader, and it may just look like spam.

**Greeting** If you normally address a person as Miss, Mrs., Dr., or Mr., then address them that way in the e-mail. If you do not know the recipient, this is also the most appropriate way to address him or her. You do not need to type, "Dear Dr. Novak"; just putting the recipient's name is appropriate. Also, never start a business e-mail with "Hey" or anything similar.

**Body** If you don't know the recipient well, you should always identify yourself in the first body paragraph. Be very clear about who you are and why you are writing. In the paragraphs that follow, get straight to the point about why you are writing, what you need, and what the next steps will be. Also, note that e-mails should never be longer than 200 words, and you should always skip lines between paragraphs.

**Signature** When contacting someone outside your own organization, you should write a signature line that includes your full name, position, organization name, and all contact information (address, phone, e-mail). You don't need "Sincerely" or any other sign-off. Your signature will do. You may choose to write "Thanks for your time," or something similar, but it is not necessary.

**Grammar** Always use standard capitalization. All-caps comes across as yelling, and no caps makes it look like you are uneducated. Also, exclamation points are never appropriate in a formal e-mail. Allow your words to make big points, not your punctuation.

## 16

Have students complete a task that requires real-world application. For example, in kindergarten, students could learn about recycling and then make art out of materials found in recycling bins. In geography, students could plan a trip to a country and research what they'd have to pack and what food they would likely eat. In math, you could provide students with the blueprints for a house and ask them to figure out exactly how much paint they would need to paint the exterior with two coats. This helps to answer the question, "Why do we need to know how to do this?"

## 17

Hey, this may be selfish, but it's a great idea. For one choice, ask students to create an assessment that could be given at the end of the unit. They could write math problems, write word problems, create a vocabulary quiz, or create their own UDL assessment. As a part of the assessment, they must also submit an answer key. You can try to sweeten the pot by choosing the best one to distribute to the class at the end of the unit. The "prize" can be that the winning students already know all the answers so they can ace it. It's a great opportunity for students to learn the curriculum and then you don't have to create the test. Students also love taking each other's tests.

## 18

One of the best choices is to allow students to create their own choice. I once observed a teacher, Paula, who didn't provide any choices but encouraged students to determine how they would express their knowledge. Paula started the lesson by identifying the learning standard and then asked students how they wanted to communicate their proficiency. She explained that they would determine their final project for *Where the Red Fern Grows* by Wilson Rawls. She explained that students could work individually or in groups, and the only requirement was that they had to challenge themselves and choose something that they were passionate about. She clarified that she trusted them to come up with ideas that were creative and would help them to delve deeper into the novel. She gave students five minutes to come up with ideas on their own before sharing with the class. Once it was time to share, she reminded students, "If you have an idea, please raise your hand because it is important that I hear you so that I can steal your ideas and make my lesson plans next year because you are always more creative than me." Almost every hand went up. Whenever a student offered an idea, Paula praised him or her for creativity and made comments such as, "That is such a neat idea. I love how you incorporated the music reviews we wrote previously." Just think, if you do it that way, you don't even need to make an assignment sheet!

## 19

If you have voice recorders or video cameras in your classroom, you can encourage students to record answers to content-related questions on audio or video. You can download files on the computer and assess them for accuracy. This is a wonderful option for students who struggle with writing. Recording themselves also gives students an opportunity to work on volume and pacing, two important speaking skills.

## 20

Lastly, although it seems boring in comparison to the previous choices, some students like traditional assessments. You can always give students the option to express their understanding in an objective multiple-choice test or an essay. Some students are so familiar with those tests that they feel confident when they are taking them. I am always surprised when I offer a traditional choice, because there are always students who choose it. Keep those students in mind, as well.

Now that you have some ideas, how do you actually create the choice assessment? Just follow the next steps. The steps are also aligned to specific UDL Guidelines and checkpoints to make implementation easier.

1. Remember, UDL is standards-based curriculum design, so you always want to start with a standard. Choose a content standard

and type it at the top of the page. This heightens the saliency of goals and objectives.

2. Decide if you will allow students to work alone, with partners, or with groups. Make that clear in the assignment directions.

3. Provide a rationale for completing the assignment. Imagine you are answering the question, "Why do we have to learn this?" Some of the students may not need this information, but it should be available nonetheless.

4. Decide on how many options you want to provide to students and consider a strategy that you will teach them so they know how to cope if they don't know which option to select. I like to provide learners with 7 options, with the 7th choice being "Roll the dice" for students who have a difficult time making choices. If you choose this method, make sure you have dice readily available. Decide on a set amount of time that students have to choose before they must try their luck.

5. Insert your assignment choices. You may want to add a super challenging option and note that it's the hardest, because this varies the level of challenge. I call it the "super challenge," and some students always pick that option just because it's the hardest. You would assume that no one would pick it, but that's never the case. Some students are overachievers and they want to prove that they can do it.

6. If you feel it would be helpful, add some scaffolding steps at the bottom of the assignment to help students who may get stuck. This provides students with coping strategies if they are having trouble getting started. To do this, just guess the types of questions students will ask you, and beat them to it.

7. Once you have this template created, you can revise it for each additional assessment. Following are two choice assessments for elementary English.

# ✔ *My Name Is Brian*—Theme Assessment

**Objective:** *Determine the theme of a story, including how characters in the story respond to challenges.*

**Rationale:** It's important to identify the themes, or central messages, in a text because these are lessons you can apply to your own life. One of the central themes in *My Name Is Brian* is overcoming challenges. All of you will face challenges in your own life, so learning about how Brian overcame the challenges may help you to overcome your own. To really examine how Brian overcame his obstacles, choose one of the following assessments.

## Choose Your Assessment (Work Alone or with a Partner)

1.  Brian overcame many challenges. In a poster, use a combination of words and images to show what he had to overcome.

2.  Create your own club. Your club will have a positive influence on school culture and will be for students who need to overcome a certain challenge (e.g., bad handwriting, kickball skills, bringing bad lunches to school). First, name your club. Then, create a list of rules that all club members will need to follow to overcome their challenge. When finished, design a T-shirt that all club members will wear.

3.  Assume the point of view of Brian and write a letter to Isabelle explaining that all people are different and she shouldn't judge them and think they are stupid because of the way they act.

4.  Create a talk-show script with Ellen interviewing Brian and Isabelle about their experiences in 5th grade. Focus on the challenges they overcame.

5.  Develop your own assessment—you must get it approved by the teacher before you begin.

6. Super challenge: Write a short research report about a celebrity, historical figure, scientist, or inventor who had to overcome challenges to become successful. (Challenges may be disability, ethnicity, gender, and so forth.)

7. Roll the dice!

## Scaffolding

While working, if you get frustrated, follow this procedure:

1. Read the assessment guidelines again.

2. Write down the questions that you have about the assessment.

3. Ask your partner or someone around you for help. Have them write their suggestions or answers on your paper. If they don't know, have them write why they are also confused.

4. If this doesn't help, raise your hand to get my attention. I will read your questions and your classmate's feedback to try to help you.

## ▶ Narrative Writing in Kindergarten

**Objective:** *Use drawing, dictating, or writing to tell a story about something that happened to you, and share how you felt about what happened.*

**Rationale:** This morning, we went on an adventure walk all around the school grounds. I want you to write a story about what you saw and did during our adventure walk so you can share it when you get home tonight. You want to make sure to share how you felt about the adventure and whether it was fun, boring, or exciting.

## Choose Your Assessment
## (Work Alone or with a Partner)

1. Draw a picture about all the things you saw on the adventure walk. You can make a poster, or you can make a book where you draw something on each page. Once you are done, you can write words beneath your picture or you can describe your picture to me.

2. Write about your favorite part of the adventure walk.

3. Take a map of the school and trace or draw where we walked, and then tell me your favorite part of the walk.

   If you can't decide, choose a number out of a hat!

## Don't Get Frustrated! Try This Instead.

- Watch the video we recorded during the adventure walk if you need a reminder of what we saw.

- Take a break at the sensory bin.

- Ask a friend for help.

---

## ▶ Practice: PLC Assignment #2

When you focus instruction on a content standard, students can be very creative about how they express their knowledge. Using the ideas in this chapter, choose one content standard you have to teach and complete a choice assessment you can use with your standard.

> **Learning outcome:** Design a choice assessment, related to a content standard, so all students can express their knowledge within their zone of proximal development.
>
> **Rationale:** Learners are more engaged when they are provided with choices. One way to do this is to design a choice assignment, aligned to a content standard. Consider how you will teach the content and give various options and then design a choice assessment that meets the outcome above. Try to provide at least 4 options.
>
> Download an assessment template from www.katienovakudl.com or create your own. A rubric is included in Appendix C if you are interested.

## ASSESSING THE CHOICE ASSESSMENT

With so many options for students to express their knowledge, you may be wondering how to assess their work. One great way to do this is to use standards-based grading. When you plan the lesson, you align it to a standard. When students complete an assessment, you need to determine if their performance exceeded, met, or failed to meet the standard. If you use standards-based reporting, you may already have a rubric in place, but if not, you may find the following options helpful.

One option is to create a grading rubric, which includes a description of work that would meet the expectations of the assessment. If the assessment doesn't meet the criteria, it receives a score of "Not Yet." This grading scale allows students to build a growth mindset, because the message is that proficiency is in their reach. The Literacy Design Collaborative (2013) has a great model of this not-yet rubric (Table 7-1) that can be adapted for your own assessment. Their website is a treasure trove of sample prompts and rubrics to guide you if you are designing writing assessments in response to text in ELA, social studies, and science.

**TABLE 7-1:** LDC Classroom Assessment Rubric for Argumentation (Adapted from Literacy Design Collaborative, 2013, p. 13)

| SCORING ELEMENTS | NOT YET | MEETS EXPECTATIONS |
|---|---|---|
| Focus | Attempts to address prompt, but lacks focus or is off-task. | Addresses the prompt and stays on task; provides a generally convincing response. |
| Reading/research | Demonstrates weak use of reading material to develop argument. | Demonstrates generally effective use of reading material to develop an argument. |
| Controlling idea | Establishes a claim, and attempts to support an argument, but is not convincing. | Establishes a credible claim, and supports an argument that is logical and generally convincing. |
| Development | Reasoning is not clear; examples or explanations are weak or irrelevant. | Develops reasoning to support claim; provides evidence from text(s) in the form of examples or explanations relevant to the argument. |
| Organization | Provides an ineffective structure; composition does not address requirements of the prompt. | Applies an appropriate text structure to address specific requirements of the prompt. |
| Conventions | Demonstrates a weak command of standard English conventions; lacks cohesion; and language and tone are not appropriate to audience and purpose. | Demonstrates a command of standard English conventions, writing is cohesive; employs language and tone appropriate to audience and purpose |

If you want to build a rubric that identifies specific criteria required in the assessment, or if you want to identify when students have exceeded expectations, you may want to adapt the rubric above. For example, if your kindergarten students were learning the importance of Independence Day, you could assess their products with the following rubric (Table 7-2).

**TABLE 7-2:** Assessment Rubric for Specific Tasks

| SCORING ELEMENTS | NOT YET (ADD COMMENTS) | MEETS EXPECTATIONS | EXCEEDS EXPECTATIONS |
|---|---|---|---|
| Controlling | Does not write/draw/dictate an accurate reason why we celebrate Independence Day. | Writes/draws/dictates one accurate reason why we celebrate Independence Day. | Writes/draws/dictates two or more reasons why we celebrate Independence Day. |
| Development | Does not write/draw/dictate a custom associated with Independence Day. | Writes/draws/dictates one custom associated with Independence Day (i.e., parade). | Writes/draws/dictates at least one custom associated with Independence Day (i.e., parade) and explains how and why the custom began. |

# CHOICE AND MULTI-TIER SYSTEM OF SUPPORTS

Providing choice isn't just for content standards. It's also a great way to provide intervention or enrichment to students. As teachers, we're supposed to vary demands and resources to optimize challenge, but sometimes it's hard to meet all student needs at once. Revising assignments, revisiting difficult concepts, and retaking tests are all valuable strategies, but teachers rarely have time to incorporate such important activities in the learning environment.

The recently adopted Every Student Succeeds Act (ESSA) calls for tiered systems of support to meet the needs of all students. Historically, tiered systems were often referred to as *RTI models (response to intervention)*, but these models were narrow, and their focus was on increasing student achievement without providing support to educators. As a result, there is no mention of RTI in the new law. Instead, the law calls for multi-tier system of supports, which they define as "a comprehensive continuum of evidence-based, systemic practices to support a rapid response to students' needs, with regular observation to facilitate data-based instructional decision-making."

Multi-tier system of supports combine the tiered practices of RTI and the value of professional learning communities (PLCs) together into a system that focuses on improving the outcomes of all students through school improvement, professional development, and collaboration among educators (Dulaney, Hallen, & Wall, 2013). Whereas RTI systems were built on a foundation of data-based decision-making, multi-tier systems enhance the one-dimensional triangle by incorporating six foundational components: problem solving, data-driven decision-making, instructional strategies, classroom management, curriculum design, and professional development (Dulaney, Hallen, & Wall, 2013). This unified system ensures that educators can rapidly respond to students' needs.

In a traditional RTI model, all students in Tier 1 receive high-quality, scientifically based instruction. Universal screening tools help to identify struggling learners who need additional support. Students who are not making progress in Tier 1 receive Tier 2 instruction in small-group settings. Tier 2 is meant to provide a limited, but targeted, support system for students who struggle to meet grade-level performance standards so they can be successful in Tier 1. Compared to Tier 2, Tier 3 is more explicit, focuses on remediation of skills, is provided for a longer duration of time, and occurs in smaller groups. Tier 3 interventions sometimes include specialized programs (i.e., Wilson reading).

To clarify these ESSA expectations for a multi-tier system of supports and how it builds on the RTI system of the past, let me present an analogy. Imagine the former RTI as a snowman—three tiers of frozen glory sitting there in the middle of your snowy backyard.

If we want our snowman to survive and remain his icy self, we have to make sure that the environment around him allows him to flourish. Remember what happened to poor Frosty when he went in the greenhouse to save Karen? That is what can happen to an RTI model when there isn't a system around to support it. Think of a culture of problem-solving, data-based decision-making, universally designed curriculum and instructional strategies, classroom management, and professional development as sub-zero weather in the arctic. If those environmental factors are missing, you're going to have a really difficult time keeping Frosty frozen. If you don't have a multi-tier system, it is difficult to support your RTI model.

If we view the multi-tier system through the lens of UDL, and align it to the requirements of the ESSA law (see Table 7-3), we can see how it's possible for all teachers to design "a comprehensive continuum of evidence-based, systemic practices to support a rapid response to students' needs, with regular observation to facilitate data-based instructional decision-making."

**TABLE 7-3:** Multi-Tier Components Aligned to ESSA Requirements

| COMPONENTS OF A MULTI-TIER SYSTEM OF SUPPORTS | ESSA REQUIREMENTS |
|---|---|
| Problem-solving and data-driven decision-making | "Providing training, technical assistance, and capacity-building in local educational agencies to assist teachers, principals, or other school leaders with selecting and implementing formative assessments, designing classroom-based assessments, and using data from such assessments to improve instruction and student academic achievement, which may include providing additional time for teachers to review student data and respond, as appropriate" (S. 1177–127). |
| Instructional strategies | Professional development activities will improve and increase teachers' "ability to analyze student work and achievement from multiple sources, including how to adjust instructional strategies, assessments, and materials based on such analysis" (S. 1177–296). |

**TABLE 7-3:** Multi-Tier Components Aligned to ESSA Requirements *CONTINUED*

| COMPONENTS OF A MULTI-TIER SYSTEM OF SUPPORTS | ESSA REQUIREMENTS |
|---|---|
| Classroom management | Professional development activities may include activities that "improve classroom management skills" (S. 1177–296) |
| Curriculum design | Grant funds are only awarded "(A) for programs described in this Act, including teacher training, curriculum development, instructional materials, or general school improvement and reform;" and "(B) to provide direct educational services that assist all students with meeting the challenging State academic standards" (S. 1121) |
| Professional development | "Providing high-quality, personalized professional development that is evidence-based, to the extent the State (in consultation with local educational agencies in the State) determines that such evidence is reasonably available, for teachers, instructional leadership teams, principals, or other school leaders, that is focused on improving teaching and student learning and achievement" (S. 1177–127) |

Using a multi-tiered system of supports empowers all educators to use student assessment data to design curriculum that meets the needs of all learners and allows them to access grade-level standards. Even when Tier 1 instruction is universally designed, there may be some students who require remediation or enrichment, but it's difficult to make time for individual interventions when other students are not struggling. So, how do you provide Tier 2 and Tier 3 support to small groups or students or individual students while others move on, without embarrassing anyone?

You just use the choice assessment template to help you to overcome this barrier. In this model, students can revisit the concepts that will be most valuable to them and you can provide small-group intervention to those students who need additional support. The key feature here is that students are given the power to make the choice. To help them make choices, you could provide them with grade printouts or their digital portfolio so they can see which strategies they need to revisit. This enhances their capacity to monitor their progress and grow as students. Students who realize they are not struggling can request enrichment activities to push them to the next level. You could have a multi-tier day weekly, biweekly, or monthly, but it's a great practice to give them frequent opportunities to monitor their own progress and make the best decisions for their own learning, and allows you an opportunity to adjust instructional strategies, assessments, and materials for small groups of students who need more support. An example follows.

## ✔ Hooray! Hooray! It's Reflection Day!

**Objective:** *Today you will review your (grade printout, portfolio, study guide, etc.) and decide which learning activity will be the best use of your time so you can be successful.*

**Rationale:** In work, in school, and in life, it's important to assess yourself and monitor your progress as you learn. Whether it's in science class, on the basketball team, or in a relationship, it's valuable to examine your strengths and weakness and make a plan to move forward. I have just given you a copy of your (grade printout, portfolio, study guide, etc.). I would like you to examine your grades to determine which concepts you are struggling with. Then, you'll have time to revisit them.

## Choose Your Learning Activity
## (You Will Work Alone)

1.  Choose one assessment you completed this year that received a grade of C or lower (check with me if you're not sure). View the exemplar or answer key for that assessment in the green binder, view the assessment rubric, and then rewrite your assessment and what you should have done differently.

2.  If you have an A or better in the course, you may choose an enrichment activity that will allow you to synthesize what we have learned and present it in a creative way. Create a goal for your enrichment project and share it with me before you begin.

3.  If you are struggling with writing in response to text and have an average below a C, I will host a small group to review concepts. In this group, you will have the opportunity to revise a response with the help of the group.

4.  Mr. Autonomous will be available in the learning center if you want some 1:1 support as you complete a task above.

## Scaffolding

While working, if you get frustrated, follow this procedure:

1.  Read your options again.

2.  Ask someone next to you for help.

3.  If this doesn't help, raise your hand to get my attention and we'll have a writing conference.

# ADDITIONAL WAYS TO OFFER CHOICE

The focus of this chapter has been on designing choices that assess student proficiency with content standards, but there are many other ways to provide students with choices in the classroom. Whether you teach kindergarten or college courses, your students will appreciate the freedom that is inherent in making choices. Just try out some of the following strategies and you'll see that they'll make a big difference in student motivation and engagement:

1. Many teachers require students to write in blue or black ink or pencil. If you're one of these teachers, ask yourself why that is a requirement in your learning environment. Is it because you correct in red? Then allow students to write in other colors. Give students the choice to write assignments using glittery sparkling pens or exciting colors, like gold or florescent blue. Remember, our job is to teach content and skills. If writing with a black pen is a barrier for some students because they don't have one or they think it's boring, then eliminate that barrier. An assignment written in pink sparkly pen still allows you to assess student work. This not only encourages students to make a choice but also allows students to use multiple tools for construction and composition. This is also true for paper choices. Giving students the option of writing on lined paper, on graph paper, or even on a napkin can increase their engagement. If your school allows students to bring their devices, allow them to complete assignments electronically.

2. Allow students to choose whether or not to work alone or collaboratively on formative assessments. Granted, on summative assessments, you'll want students to work alone, but collaboration is an important step in scaffolding for some students. Giving students the opportunity to choose to work with a partner minimizes the threat of completing difficult assignments and encourages choice. Some students may prefer to work alone, and that's all right, too.

3. If you allow students to work in groups, consider allowing them to pick their own groups. Granted, every teacher wants to prevent

any student from feeling left out, but you could start the lesson by giving students tips on how to include each other and to not make classmates feel left out. Being able to navigate group membership is a skill that many adults haven't figured out. Teach students about being respectful and inclusive before breaking them up. Often, a gentle reminder such as "If you see someone without a group, invite them into yours immediately" prevents many issues.

4.  Often, when presenting new material to students, teachers present to the whole class. Another option is to allow students to choose how they want to learn the information. Instead of one presentation with visual, audio, and tactile components, you could separate the representation portion of the lesson into stations and allow students to learn in the way that is most advantageous to them. For example, you may have an article that some students could read, while others can watch a film on a tablet. Still others could sit with the teacher for a mini-lecture with notes.

5.  Some teachers allow students to choose their seats. In high school, one of my teachers used to say, "You can sit where you like if I like where you sit." You don't want students to distract each other, but you also want them to feel comfortable in the seat they choose. If student distraction becomes a problem, you have to remove the barrier, but students could be given a chance to decide where to sit. If you've ever been to a wedding, you know what I'm talking about. You scour the table looking for your place card with the table number and then recklessly try to find the cards of all your besties, hoping you're at the same table. The same is true for the kids.

6.  If letting students choose their seats doesn't work in your room, allow them to choose seats in a more literal sense. Some teachers have standard desks while others have café-style tables with different types of chairs. I've seen classrooms with beanbag chairs, benches, stools, exercise balls, and even couches. You can always find free furniture on sites like Craigslist.com, so start shopping. Having options that allow students to be comfortable can make a big difference in their engagement.

# SUMMARY

When teaching content standards, there are no specific methods that have to be followed. Students need to express their knowledge, but there is no prescribed way within the standard. This allows teachers to provide students with various choices that will engage them in the learning process. This can be used throughout the year as formative or summative assessments to quantify student understanding of difficult topics. Student choice can also be provided when revisiting concepts using your district multi-tier system. Choice not only engages students, but it increases motivation and value.

# DISCUSSION QUESTIONS

1.  How does student choice relate to student engagement?

2.  How does the new ESSA provide you with more choices as you implement multi-tier systems in your classroom environment?

3.  How does choice relate to engagement in your own teaching practice? Do you feel more or less engaged when you're required to teach certain content in specific ways?

4.  Can you think of any additional choices you could offer to students? If so, what are they?

# 8

# Scaffolding

## Setting the Bar High and Raising Students to It

We've all heard the ridiculous adage, "Those who can't, teach." I once saw someone wearing a T-shirt with that saying on it. I should have invited him back to my classroom to deal with 12- and 13-year-olds all day. That would've taught him the definition of the word "can't." Being an educator is a calling, not a backup plan.

Teachers are born with a natural curiosity, patience, creativity, and a passion for learning. Many of us probably chose to become teachers because learning was something we enjoyed. This is not true for some of our students. There are countless reasons why students don't enjoy school, but one of the reasons why students struggle is because school isn't something they are good at.

Subjects across the content area are built on the cornerstones of

**Objective:** *You will be able to create scaffolded assignments for your methods standards to engage students and facilitate personal coping strategies when it comes to specific tasks.*

**Rationale:** The state curriculum standards requires students to read and write across the curriculum, yet few teachers break down and teach the skills necessary to be successful at these tasks. With only 38 percent of 8th graders proficient at reading, it becomes necessary to scaffold important skills for students so they can internalize and transfer them. This chapter outlines scaffolding strategies that can be used in your learning environment and provides templates for assignments that require scaffolding.

literacy, reading and writing, yet less than half of the 8th graders in the country are proficient readers. If we want students to succeed as learners, we have to teach them to think, read, write, speak, and listen. We can't assume students already have these skills, regardless of their age or perceived ability level. Some kids become really good at faking academic skills, and that's not fair to them. We have to teach them *how to learn*, and to do that, we have to break the skills down into manageable steps.

As a quick review, effective scaffolded instruction has four key features: active engagement, intersubjectivity, ongoing diagnosis, and transfer of responsibility (Puntambekar & Hübscher, 2005). *Active engagement* is when teachers are fully involved in helping students construct knowledge. *Intersubjectivity* is the symbiotic relationship between you and your students. *Ongoing diagnosis* reminds teachers to consistently provide students with feedback. Lastly, *transfer of responsibility* is key because ultimately students must complete work independently, but they can't start the process alone.

Let's start by breaking down a scaffolded lesson and aligning it to the UDL Guidelines and the four key features of scaffolded instruction so it's clear that scaffolding and UDL are practically interchangeable.

I once observed a brilliant teacher named Tara. Tara began her lesson by explaining to the students that they would read two different selections about monkeys and that the ultimate objective of the lesson was to write a text-based response comparing and contrasting the two selections, one fiction and one non-fiction (Provide options for executive functions; Provide options for sustaining effort and persistence). Each student would complete the text-based response independently for homework. Tara started by giving a short lecture on the differences between fiction and non-fiction (Provide options for perception; Provide options for comprehension). There was a chart in the front of the room that students could copy into their notebooks, and she showed a short video clip on the differences (Provide options for perception). Students were encouraged to go to the front of the room to get a closer look at the chart if necessary. When she was finished with the representation portion of the lesson, students read two selections. The first selection, *Why Monkeys Live in*

*Trees*, by Julius Lester, was fiction. Students had to read this selection silently, but only after Tara pre-taught the difficult vocabulary in the story (Provide options for language). The three words she reviewed were *bellowed*, *reflection*, and *regal*. She activated prior knowledge by reminding the students that both *bellowed* and *reflection* were in the previous story (Provide options for comprehension). She made a joke about bellowing after eating a hot pepper, and the entire class burst into laughter. Her connection with the students and their knowledge was evident, and this relates to the concept of intersubjectivity. Also, she was actively involved in their learning throughout the process.

The class then moved on to read *The Case of the Monkeys That Fell from the Trees*, by Susan Quinlan. Tara read the excerpt aloud and stopped periodically to allow students to think-pair-share using inferential questions, comparing the non-fiction piece to the previous fiction selection (Provide options for executive functions; Provide options for sustaining effort and persistence). A question was posed, and then students were able to think about the answer, find a partner, and share their answers. Then, they shared answers with the class, and Tara gave them feedback or provided ongoing diagnosis. They had to discuss the differences in the selection until they agreed upon the answers. When both selections were finished, students were given a graphic organizer to help them begin planning the open response (Provide options for executive functions). They could work in groups to plan the graphic organizer (Provide options for sustaining effort and persistence; Provide options for expression and communication), but each student was responsible for completing the response independently for homework. By doing this, Tara was beginning to transfer the responsibility to the students. At the end of the class, Tara made a circuit around the room and gave each student feedback on their graphic organizer (Provide options for sustaining effort and persistence; Provide options for self-regulation) so they were prepared to go home and complete the assessment on the two selections. Because she used the four key features of scaffolding and UDL principles, students were confident that they could return home and complete the assessment.

As you can see, Tara's lesson started with teacher-led support and transitioned to working with peers, and ultimately, students were expected to complete work independently. This independent work, however, was not a threat to students, as they received graphic organizers, had an opportunity to work with peers, and received mastery-oriented feedback before going home to work alone. That's what scaffolding is about. Successful teachers teach lessons with explicit scaffolding where responsibility for learning is gradually released to students.

# SCAFFOLDED READING

The Every Student Succeeds Act (ESSA) identifies key components of comprehensive literacy instruction, all of which align to the UDL Framework. In Subpart 2—Literacy Education for All, Results for the Nation (S. 1177–135) the term *comprehensive literacy instruction* is defined as instruction that:

A. "includes developmentally appropriate, contextually explicit, and systematic instruction, and frequent practice, in reading and writing across content areas;

B. includes age-appropriate, explicit, systematic, and intentional instruction in phonological awareness, phonic decoding, vocabulary, language structure, reading fluency, and reading comprehension;

C. includes age-appropriate, explicit instruction in writing, including opportunities for children to write with clear purposes, with critical reasoning appropriate to the topic and purpose, and with specific instruction and feedback from instructional staff;

D. makes available and uses diverse, high-quality print materials that reflect the reading and development levels, and interests, of children;

E. uses differentiated instructional approaches, including individual and small group instruction and discussion;

**F.** provides opportunities for children to use language with peers and adults in order to develop language skills, including developing vocabulary;

**G.** includes frequent practice of reading and writing strategies;

**H.** uses age-appropriate, valid, and reliable screening assessments, diagnostic assessments, formative assessment processes, and summative assessments to identify a child's learning needs, to inform instruction, and to monitor the child's progress and the effects of instruction;

**I.** uses strategies to enhance children's motivation to read and write and children's engagement in self-directed learning;

**J.** incorporates the principles of universal design for learning;

**K.** depends on teachers' collaboration in planning, instruction, and assessing a child's progress and on continuous professional learning; and

**L.** links literacy instruction to the challenging State academic standards, including the ability to navigate, understand, and write about, complex print and digital subject matter."

In this definition, we see many of the concepts we've unpacked throughout the text, including differentiated instructional approaches, engagement, self-directed learning, professional learning, and the importance of aligning instruction with state academic standards. It's like a UDL advertisement!

Regardless of the subject or level you teach, state academic standards place an emphasis on literacy instruction in all subject areas, which may feel a little overwhelming to teachers without English and reading backgrounds, but reading is necessary in all subject areas if students are to have improved literacy.

When teaching reading comprehension, you need to consider the three main principles of UDL. First, you need to make it clear *why* they are reading. Next, you need to teach students *how* to read critically, and lastly, in order to be engaged, students need to know *what* they are going to read. To do this, you need to present the text to students in ways that are accessible to them. Giving students a purpose makes work more meaningful.

Regardless of what you teach, students need to read. They may not read in a traditional sense, but they need to read. "Reading" music and artwork are both important skills that need to be taught. "Reading" a math textbook is imperative for success in math. As teachers, we are collectively responsible for literacy. Students need to read to become better readers, writers, thinkers, and speakers so they can be successful lifelong learners.

Not only are students expected to read in all content areas, but research also has shown that all students should be reading texts that are difficult enough to challenge their existing language knowledge (Indrisano & Chall, 1995) because these texts prepare them to take high-stakes exams. To pass high-stakes exams, students must read at or above grade level. Students must also be able to comprehend and respond to challenging text so that they can graduate from high school and pursue careers that interest them. Now, are the high-stakes exams the most important assessments in the world? Absolutely not, but students need to do well on them to move forward. We owe them reading instruction so they can be successful, regardless of how we feel about the test. In order for students to learn how to read, we need to scaffold effective reading strategies. This is second nature for reading teachers, but literacy is now a shared skill.

First, all teachers should understand the basic text structures because knowledge of these structures is necessary for students to comprehend and make predictions about difficult text. Second, it's helpful if all teachers are aware of the strategies used by proficient readers so they can model them for students. What follows is an explanation of text structures and common reading strategies so you can incorporate them in your reading instruction.

# Text Structures

In 4th grade, students move from learning to read to reading to learn. Before 4th grade, students often read a lot of fiction. These stories follow the simple plot structure shown here. They become familiar with this structure. The structure is predictable so students can learn to read.

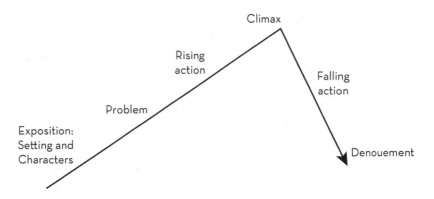

After 4th grade, materials become increasingly expository, and students must read to learn. This lag has been called "the 4th grade slump" (Indrisano & Chall, 1995). The problem at this point is that students are familiar with only one text structure. They need to learn the characteristics of expository text, as well as the structures authors use to organize the text.

All students need to understand that expository text is subject-oriented and focuses on a specific topic. These texts use multiple organizational structures, and unlike stories, expository texts are too difficult to predict based on content. Predictions must be based on organizational structure.

Teaching text structure can help students become aware of the patterns and structures that are used in expository texts so they can anticipate the kind of information that will be presented and make predictions about the text.

# Expository Text Structure

There are six main text structures that authors use to organize expository, or informational, text. Knowledge of the structures allows students to highlight the critical features of each structure and make predictions. The expository text structures are description, sequencing, compare and contrast, cause and effect, problem and solution, and question and answer:

**Description**  When an author uses description, the reader expects the writer to tell characteristics. When reading a description, proficient readers will ask, "What are you describing?" or "What are some of the qualities of this concept?"

**Sequencing**  When an author uses sequencing structures, readers expect that events will be told in the order they happened. Sequencing structures include both chronological order and sequential order. While reading sequencing structures, readers ask, "What is going to happen next?" or "What is the next step in this sequence?" Recipes, how-to manuals, and lab reports are written in sequential order.

**Compare and contrast**  In compare-and-contrast texts, readers expect to learn how one thing is like or different from another thing or things. While reading, students may ask, "What are the similar and different qualities of these things?" A helpful graphic representation to use when reading compare and contrast is the Venn diagram.

**Cause and effect**  Cause-and-effect texts discuss the effect of one thing on another or why an effect takes place. A question that helps readers determine the main idea of cause-and-effect texts is, "What are the causes and effects of this event?"

**Problem and solution**  In a problem-and-solution text, a reader expects to identify a problem, predict a solution, and learn how viable that solution is and how it will be implemented.

**Question and answer**  The last text structure, which is very simple to identify, is question and answer, which is just that. This is like a Dear Abby article where the reader considers a question and then an answer is given. Often, the question is in bold or italics.

Once you are familiar with expository text structure, you can represent that knowledge to students. It may be helpful to pre-teach important transitional words that signal important information or a shift in focus and establish the text structure. This will allow students to ask appropriate questions about the text, which will increase their comprehension. So, how do you teach text structure? The sequential structure here outlines the process for you:

1. Provide explicit instruction. For example, model specifically how and when to use strategies, such as attending to signal words, while reading different content areas or when writing expository text.

2. Scaffold instruction. Help students by providing clues and supports as they attempt to identify the text structures in various texts. One clue might be to provide students with examples of situations where these text structures are most commonly used or to provide them with a reading guide or a literacy trekker—you can find directions on how to create one in this chapter. You may want to allow students to work in groups to discuss the text structure or facilitate a Paideia Seminar so students can critically discuss the use of signal words and how they relate to the structure.

3. Use and create graphic organizers for each text structure. You can create these graphic organizers with students or find some great ones online. If students are familiar with the graphic organizers, they can create them on their own as soon as they identify a text structure, and this will allow them to determine the main idea of the text.

## Reading Strategies

"Reading" does not mean simply decoding words. Many students can decode a text and comprehend little or nothing. To read is to absorb and interact with ideas. Interacting with a book is like interacting with a living, breathing being. It can speak to you, share ideas, inspire you, or infuriate you. Just as human beings need to learn social and people skills to develop relationships, students need to learn reading skills to have a relationship with the text. Proficient readers inherently know how to interact with the text, but for some students, these strategies need to be scaffolded so they are accessible. If you are reading this, you already know these strategies, even if you don't realize it. McEwan (2007) outlines seven strategies that are important to scaffold with students when they are reading. These strategies relate to the definition of literacy in the ESSA and the UDL Guidelines because they provide students with options for comprehension.

Students need explicit instruction in reading before they can become independent readers. When students are first reading in your class, you should model several strategies. The first is *activating prior knowledge*. Knowledge is like a magnet, so students need to know where new information fits into their current understanding. Remind students what they already know about a topic to prepare them. Also, activate a purpose for reading to begin to engage students from the beginning. Why are they reading a particular text? Understanding this also helps them to construct meaning. At this time, it may be helpful to present the text structure to students to help them to predict what they will be reading next. Without a previous knowledge of text structure, this task will be difficult to impossible while reading.

The second strategy is making *inferences*. The text has explicit language, but there is also information that students must infer or assume. This "reading between the lines" can be modeled to students when you're reading aloud. You can model the metacognitive strategy of stopping and asking questions about the text to make assumptions. Reading closely requires multiple readings of the same text, so modeling this process helps students see that making inferences doesn't happen easily or automatically. When writing text-based responses, it's also important for students to cite text. When you ask students to support their conclusions, it's good practice to ask them to ground the discussion by citing textual evidence. It's also important at this point to relate back to any prior knowledge they have that will help them to fill in the blanks in their inference.

Proficient readers are constantly *monitoring and clarifying* the text. In short, they are thinking while they are reading. They may ask questions or reread excerpts to make certain they comprehend what they are reading. They don't just keep reading when things get confusing. If they get to a portion of the text that isn't accessible, they need to slow down and try to figure out when they lost their understanding and why. They also need to search for connections in the text, which may not be obvious on a first reading.

Good readers *ask questions*. They may ask comprehension questions about the text, or they may ask questions about how the new content fits in with previous texts. Students need to know that reading is like a conversation, and it's not one-sided. Authors embed answers to questions that are hidden in the inherent structure of a text. If an author uses a problem/solution text structure, the questions "What is the problem?" and "What are possible solutions?" and "What is the best solution?" and "How will the solution be implemented?" beg to be asked. Asking and answering questions about a text is an important skill for all students.

Reading and analyzing authors' opinions and arguments helps to build critical thinking skills in students. One cannot evaluate an argument without asking questions about the relevance and reliability of the evidence. Teaching students to question the validity of what they read is an important skill as they move forward in life. This is also necessary for students to "assess how point of view or purpose shapes the content and style of a text." Students must be taught how to analyze an author's purpose before reading their intended message.

Some students want to read a text once and be done with it, but comprehension doesn't work like osmosis. Readers have to *search the text* to find answers to questions, determine how context clues help to define unfamiliar vocabulary, and clarify misinterpretations in the text. It may be a stretch, but stress to students that literacy and education are gifts that millions of people in the world would love to have. A text is like a gold mine. You don't just give the area a quick once over, because you'd be missing a lot of gold. You need to dig in, search around, and discover every kernel of knowledge hidden in the text. This is what close reading is all about.

Reading is mental work, and many students don't want to persevere and put this work in. It's hard. Think of yourself as a coach, and show them that although it's hard work, it pays off. This is a valuable skill, especially on standardized tests. Often on reading comprehension tests, students are expected to return to the text to search for answers, but they rely on their memory and fail to go back and do the work. If they don't return, they haven't truly read a word. This is especially important when students have to interpret words and phrases as they are used in a text. The meaning of words don't just pop out at the reader, nor does the author's tone. Students need to learn to search through the text to find clues and textual evidence to help them interpret the meaning of unfamiliar words.

*Summarizing*, or *paraphrasing*, is an important skill that all readers should be able to use. If students can't put the text in their own words in an objective summary, then they don't truly understand what they have read. To summarize text, students need to use the previous strategies, such as activating prior knowledge and searching the text for context clues and transition words to help to identify the text structure. Together, these strategies will help students put the text in their own words.

Lastly, students should practice *visualizing* as they are reading. Language allows us to paint pictures in our heads or create graphic organizers where we can make information fit together in a logical way. This is especially important for visual learners. You may have students in your class who need the concrete image to put the information in the text together. Teaching the text structures discussed previously allows students to visualize a text.

Used together, these strategies help readers to comprehend what is in the text and will help you to align your curriculum to your standards. Again, you can't just provide the strategies and expect students to use them. These skills have to be modeled and practiced multiple times before students can use them independently. Teaching the skills, however, is time well spent. If your students aren't proficient readers, they are wasting time staring at text that may be meaningless to them. Teach them to make meaning.

When modeling these critical reading skills, it may be helpful to use both shared reading and close reading with your students. Shared reading is an instructional strategy based on a scaffolded model of learning. In shared reading, a teacher demonstrates how reading works—the skills, strategies, and behaviors of good readers (Routman, 2003). Often during shared reading, a group of learners observes an expert (that's you!) reading a piece of text with fluency and expression, and is invited to read along. Through teacher modeling, students join to read the text collaboratively. In this model, students can read the text multiple times to build confidence, fluency, and word familiarity, although it is not required. During these readings, teachers may also demonstrate their thinking, and guide and support that discussion with students to help demonstrate metacognitive thinking.

Close reading is the process by which students reread a text multiple times to extract multiple levels of meaning. When students are close reading, they focus on the central ideas and key supporting details, reflect on the meanings of individual words and sentences, and observe the development of ideas over the course of the text. To bring student attention to the most important aspects of the text, teachers may prompt students to ask themselves questions about the context, the craft and structure, and the integration of knowledge and ideas in the text. Boyles (2013), author of *Closing In on Close Reading*, suggests the following questions to begin:

- What is the author telling me here?

- Are there any hard or important words?

- What does the author want me to understand?

- How does the author play with language to add to meaning?

Once students have an understanding of the basic concepts in the text, they can move on to subsequent readings to examine deeper questions.

Based on the analysis above, the two concepts are related, but different. Shared reading is an instructional strategy where teachers build students' reading fluency by offering graduated levels of support. Close reading, in contrast, is a process where students read and reread text to delve deeper into the meaning. When you want to model scaffolding with rigorous text, you can use shared reading to model close reading with your students.

If you have early elementary students, you can scaffold this reading by using visual literacy. *Picture This: Visual Literacy as a Pathway to Character*

*Understanding* (Prior, Willson, and Martinez, 2012), provides tips of scaffolding reading using visual text. Students do not only read verbal text, they also read visual text. Students can learn a lot about characters from artistic devices that illustrators use to develop plot, setting, and character. When teachers become "curators" and draw students' attention to pictorial content such as characters' facial expressions and pictorial devices such as color, line, size, and texture, they are highlighting patterns and guiding visualization, which helps students make inferences from the text.

So, next time you prepare a shared reading, read with an eye toward the art, and model this for students so that you support their decoding of text. Ask questions like the following and encourage students to discuss their interpretations to foster collaboration and community.

- What do you see in this picture? What does it mean to you?

- What colors are used? What do the colors say about the characters or setting?

- Where is the character placed on the page? What might this say about the character?

- What can we learn from the facial expressions or the posture of the character?

Teaching visual literacy paves the path to reading comprehension as students learn that there are endless clues embedded in the text. Starting this process early will help students maximize transfer by learning to read verbal text closely.

## Putting It All Together: The Literacy Trekker

After teaching about text structure and reading strategies, one great way to bring student attention to the most important aspects of the text is to create a map to help them read a passage, called a *literacy trekker*. The literacy trekker acts as a guide for students who are reading important text and models for them what good readers do when they are reading. Think of a literacy trekker as a document that scaffolds shared reading strategies as students engage in close reading.

Clearly you cannot create one of these for every passage, but they are worthwhile when students are studying important content that you will build on in future lessons. This is also a great strategy to use when students will ultimately write a response to text.

Some reasons why you should create literacy trekkers:

- They encourage students to be active and thoughtful readers.

- They activate students' prior knowledge.

- They teach students to monitor their understanding of the text as they're reading.

- They help strengthen reading and critical thinking skills.

- They help students to identify text structure.

To create a literacy trekker, use these steps as a guide:

1. Determine the text to be used and pre-select points where the students should pause during the reading process (Every page? Every section?). This doesn't have to be traditional text. It could also be a sheet of music or a painting to analyze.

2. Remember to start with the *why*. Define a reading goal. Ask yourself why the students are reading and be sure that the goal is connected to a curriculum standard. What is the most important content? State this purpose to students. For example, "You will identify three times Dally shows courage in *The Outsiders* and infer why his actions were so courageous."

3. Pre-reading prompts: Direct and activate students' thinking prior to reading a passage by prompting them to scan or write the title, chapter headings, illustrations, and other materials that will be important. Begin with an open-ended question to direct students as they make predictions about the content or perspective of the text or activate prior knowledge. Some examples:

    - What does courage mean to you? What is the most courageous thing you have ever done?

- What are the steps in the scientific method?

- In the last unit, we discussed the concept of slope. Define slope in your own words.

- Describe to someone who does not know what the differences are between the area and the circumference of a circle.

4. Have students read up to the first pre-selected stopping point. Then prompt students to complete an activity.

    a. Ask questions.

    b. Have them define key words. Provide students with dictionaries or have them write the most important words they have read. You could also bring students' attention to important context clues.

    c. Ask students to interact with text. Can they make a connection personally? Does it remind them of something else? Prompt them to ask questions or make connections at certain points. Think back to the reading strategies when asking questions.

    d. Ask students to draw a picture, write any questions they have, or devise other strategies to improve visualization.

    e. Always scaffold an example answer if you ask a question so students know what an appropriate response looks like.

    f. At the end, ask students to identify the text structure. It may help to provide a word bank with transition words. Ask them to identify words that helped them identify the structure.

This process should be continued until students have read each section of the passage, looked at each picture, and solved each problem.

Following is a sample literacy trekker. Note how the trekker activates students' prior knowledge, models comprehension strategies, and guides students' attention to the most important concepts in the text.

# ✔ Literacy Trekker on *The Outsiders*

**Standards:**

*Cite several pieces of textual evidence to support analysis of what the text says explicitly, as well as inferences drawn from the text.*

*Analyze how particular elements of a story interact (e.g., how the setting shapes and characters or plot).*

After reading pages 91–96, you will complete a text-based question that asks you to identify ways that Dally showed courage when rushing into the church.

Before reading, do the following:

1. The definition of courage is the quality of being brave: the ability to face danger, difficulty, uncertainty, or pain without being overcome by fear or being deflected from a chosen course of action. What does courage mean to you?

2. Read pg. 91 and then (STOP). On pg. 91, we learn that Pony and Johnny are in the burning church. What do you think Dally is going to do? Why?

3. After answering the previous questions, begin reading at the top of pg. 92. Read to the bottom of pg. 93 and then (STOP). Describe the setting of the church. How does Pony describe the condition it's in? Use at least 2 quotes from the text. Hint: Look at the top of pg. 93.

4. Draw the scene from the church as you visualize it. Use color. Think about why you're making the artistic choices you are making. We will discuss this as a group.

5. Now, read from the top of pg. 94 to the bottom of pg. 95. (STOP) Why don't you think the other bystanders (people who were watching) went in the church?

## ▶ Practice: PLC Assignment #3

**Objective:** *Create a product that will scaffold important reading skills for a particular passage.*
*The document should help students to highlight important features and content of the text, highlight reading strategies and standards, and allow them to monitor their progress.*

**Rationale:** Many students have difficulty with reading comprehension. In fact, in the 2008 Nation's Report Card, it was reported that less than 40% of students read at grade level. Literacy is so important that it is now every teacher's responsibility to help students read (whether that means to read traditional text, music, artwork, math textbooks, and so on). In this project, you will create a document to help guide students through a "reading" passage. There should be checkpoints to bring student attention to the most important content and to check comprehension. This document should model reading strategies so students could transfer the skills and apply the same strategies when they read independently. Ideally, you would create a literacy trekker for any text that is particularly important for students to understand.

**Option:** If you have students who are already proficient readers, you may prefer to ask them to create a literacy trekker that highlights their reading process. You can ask them to identify where they stopped, what questions they asked themselves, what connections they made during the text, and which strategies they used to comprehend difficult vocabulary. Students can then collaborate with classmates to share their process and dive deeper into the close reading of text.

# SCAFFOLDED WRITING

Writing is a complex process with multiple steps. It's not enough to present the writing process to students. Rather, you need to model each step and have frequent check-ins with students to ensure understanding and ensure that students can sustain effort and persist. Students are more likely to be successful if exemplars and rubrics are provided as options.

Also, the best writing is rewriting, so allowing time for revisions may increase student writing proficiency.

The writing process includes multiple steps: brainstorming, drafting, revising, editing, and publishing. If your students struggle with writing, you may want to scaffold each step of the process until students can move through the steps independently.

# Brainstorming

Before students begin to write, they need to select an idea. To help them come up with an idea, provide them with a rationale for the assignment. Knowing why they are writing will help them to feel more in control of the process and will help to define the parameters of possible topics.

**Example:** Assignment rationale for 6th-grade Social Studies unit

Being able to express your opinion and get others to agree with you is an important skill in school and in life. It's also important to support your opinion with facts and information. In this assignment, you will assume the point of view of an early explorer trying to convince your friends to come with you to America. You may choose an explorer we learned about in the text, or you can pretend that you went back in time and were one of the explorers. You will need to complete your research about the benefits of immigrating before drafting your persuasive letter.

Once you review the rationale together, model the type of thinking you do before selecting a topic. Do you make a list? Do you use a graphic organizer? Provide students with multiple graphic organizers and tips so they feel prepared to select an idea. You could also provide students with a list of possible topics if they have trouble selecting one. In the previous example, you could provide students with a list of all the early explorers you learned about in class. After this step, check in with students to ensure their selections will allow them to be successful. This graduated support will ensure that students don't begin writing about a topic that will not allow them to be successful.

# Drafting

This is when students write their first draft, but they can't do this until they know how to organize the writing assignment. Depending on the type of writing, you'll need to provide students with an exemplar so they have at least one model of an appropriate length and complexity and see how it will be organized. Different writing tasks have different requirements, so you need to make it very clear if there are parameters in the assignment. Is there a minimum page count or word count? Students will ask these questions, so if your assessment has requirements, make those clear to students. To help students become self-directed learners, it is helpful to communicate the criteria for success so they know the rules before they begin to break them.

Think of a scaffolded support document as a recipe. Although pastry chefs don't walk around with Betty Crocker's cookbook, they all seem to know that to make pastry one has to mix flour, water, and shortening in pretty exact ratios. Don't know the basic formula? Well, you're likely to end up with dough that is too sticky or too crumbly. So, how are they masters of pastry without a recipe? Here's the answer: every recipe is in their head, and it's built off that original recipe they made in their grandmother's kitchen using good ol' Betty Crocker.

Following is an example of how this concept of a recipe can be used to help elementary students write their letter as early explorers. Note that you wouldn't need to provide this information throughout the year, but when you are beginning to scaffold instruction, you will want to make all requirements clear to students so they will be able to replicate the strategies on their own.

---

## ✔ Assignment Organization

Name: Write your name here.

Date: Write the date we begin the assignment.

### Introduction Paragraph

First sentence: Use a hook. Types of hooks: sensory detail or simile, question, quote.

Sentences 2–4: This is where you will forecast the information that will be in the following body paragraphs. For example, you may note that there is religious freedom in America. Do not say, "In the following paragraphs, I will tell you about..."

Last sentence: Thesis—the point of your essay. This should be one sentence about what you're trying to convince your friends to do. You may use the following sentence to help you: "After reading this letter, you should want to come with me because _____."

## Paragraphs 2–4: Body Paragraphs

This is where you will provide logically ordered reasons why your friends should come with you to America. Try to use a lot of facts from your textbook in every paragraph. Every opinion must relate back to textual evidence.

Paragraph 2: One logical reason why your friends should come with you (e.g., religious freedom).

Paragraph 3: Another logical reason why your friends should come with you.

Paragraph 4: Another logical reason why your friends should come with you.

## Conclusion Paragraph

Restate the thesis—this is from your introduction paragraph. Don't copy it exactly, but make it similar.

Next, start with the transition, "In the future..." and then use 3–5 examples of foreshadowing (foreshadowing is providing hints about what will happen in the future), where you warn what could happen if you friends don't come with you.

## Steps to Follow If You're Overwhelmed

1.  Get a piece of paper and a writing utensil from the student resource center or take out your device.

2.  If you are stuck, start with the body paragraphs, which will include the reasons why someone should immigrate to America. We will have already discussed this in class, so this would be a good place to start. You can always come back to the introduction later. If you are writing your draft on paper, leave at least a half of a page for you to write your introduction later.

3.  After writing your body paragraphs, if you are unable to write the introduction or conclusion, write a list of specific questions you have about how to begin. Do not write, "I don't know how to write an introduction or conclusion." What exactly is confusing?

4.  Once you have written your body paragraphs and have a list of questions about the introduction and conclusion, you may raise your hand and call me over.

As you can see, the previous template outlines the expectations of the assignment. Many students will not need such specific scaffolding, but it should be available to them regardless. Again, you may not use this on summative assessments because if you scaffold correctly, students will come to understand how to organize the letter and will be able to transfer that knowledge to future assignments. Regardless of what grade you teach, however, students should have the opportunity to understand exactly what is expected of them. This is why it is important to also provide students with rubrics before they draft their writing assignments.

If you use the language in your standards as you design your rubrics, you may find it valuable to teach the rubric. Have students examine past student work and grade assignments based on the rubric. For an entire week, the rubric can be your curriculum. After that, students have a much better understanding of how they can use the rubric to self-evaluate. To reinforce this, offer students prizes, like stickers or candy, if they can grade their own paper on the rubric and score within one point of your own score. After a few months, all students can use the rubric with their own papers. By the end of the year, many students can write an A paper because they finally know what one is. For each assignment, you may choose to create one of the "not yet" rubrics, or if you want to define criteria for multiple proficiency levels, you may create a rubric like the following. Following is a rubric for the explorer letter:

| | NOT YET | MEETS EXPECTATIONS | EXCEEDS EXPECTATIONS |
|---|---|---|---|
| Introduction | The introduction either does not orient the reader by introducing the narrator, or does not organize the events that will unfold in the body. | The introduction orients the reader by introducing the narrator, and organizes the events that will unfold in the body, but the hook lacks creativity. | The introduction orients the reader by introducing the narrator, and organizes the events that will unfold in the body. The intro is also memorable because the hook engages the reader. |
| Organization | Opinions and reasons are not linked together using transitional words or phrases. | Opinions and reasons are linked together using some transitional words and phrases, but they are simple transition words. | Opinions and reasons are linked together using advanced transition words (e.g., *consequently*, *specifically*). The letter does not rely on simple transition words like *first*, *next*, and *then*. |

|  | NOT YET | MEETS EXPECTATIONS | EXCEEDS EXPECTATIONS |
|---|---|---|---|
| Foreshadowing | Use of foreshadowing in the conclusion is not historically accurate, but attempts are made to make it persuasive. | Use of foreshadowing in the conclusion is historically accurate, but only minimally persuasive. | Use of foreshadowing in the conclusion is historically accurate and is very persuasive to the reader. |
| Information from text | Few of your opinions and reasons are historically accurate. | Most opinions and reasons are historically accurate and well researched in the social studies text. | All opinions and reasons are historically accurate and well researched, in the social studies text, and beyond. |
| Language conventions | Letter contains errors that interfere with meaning. | Grammar is accurate; few errors in spelling and punctuation that do not interfere with meaning. | Grammar is consistently accurate, and punctuation is accurate; no typographical errors. |

## Revising and Editing

This is the longest process because it requires students to rework the draft of their essays to ensure that they have met all assignment guidelines. The rubric is a great tool to help students, but it's also important to meet with students to give them mastery-oriented feedback on how they can improve their writing before they turn it in for a grade.

Many writers confuse revision and editing. While revising is focused on the reworking of content, task, and purpose, editing is often associated with the overall content and structure of the text. Both revision and editing may involve rewriting and take a significant amount of time, so scaffolding is imperative. To do this well, provide students with a revision/editing checklist, like the one below, and encourage them to collaborate with peers to improve their work until they understand what to look for when they revise and edit their work.

| CONTENT AND DEVELOPMENT | FOCUS AND ORGANIZATION | EFFECTIVE SENTENCES | WORD CHOICE | GRAMMAR, USAGE, AND MECHANICS |
|---|---|---|---|---|
| You need one clear main idea, supported with details. You must sum up the main idea in a thesis. Highlight thesis in intro and conclusion in pink. | Intro has a hook, some background information, and a thesis statement that address the prompt. | Sentences must vary in length. To determine this, count words. If you have many short sentences, combine them to be compound or complex. | Aim to replace at least 20 words in the essay. Try not to repeat any words throughout the essay. | Correct spelling— use the dictionary. |
| Use at least 20 specific sensory details or specific details from the text. If you use sensory details, the reader should have a strong visual image in every paragraph. | In an essay, your body paragraphs should follow the order of your thesis. Use transitions for each paragraph that are subtle. Don't just say, "The second reason you should come to America is..." | Start sentences in many different ways. Circle the first word in each sentence. If any words repeat in a given paragraph, revise. If you are using dialogue, read it aloud to see if it is something someone would actually say. | Use vivid verbs. Get rid of words like *walk*, *said*, and *like*, and choose more accurate verbs. | Correct capitalization. Sentences all start with capital letters. All titles and proper nouns are capitalized. |
| Every paragraph must relate back to the thesis. If it doesn't, make a connection clear. | The conclusion must restate the thesis and may pose a question for future thought or can include a detail from the introduction to tie up the essay. | Compound sentences must use a coordinating conjunction: *for, and, nor, but, or, yet,* and *so.* Make sure you have a variety of them throughout the essay. | Replace common nouns with proper nouns whenever possible. For example, change *the ship* to *the Mayflower.* | If you use two adjectives to describe something, put a comma between them. Here's an example: He was a fat, brown dog. |

| CONTENT AND DEVELOPMENT | FOCUS AND ORGANIZATION | EFFECTIVE SENTENCES | WORD CHOICE | GRAMMAR, USAGE, AND MECHANICS |
|---|---|---|---|---|
| Use original details that are beyond the obvious. Say things in ways other people wouldn't think about saying them. This is your voice. | Intro and conclusion are a minimum of four sentences. Body paragraphs are a minimum of seven. | Actually read the essay aloud to yourself to make sure all sentences flow smoothly. | Imagery, imagery, imagery... almost all your words should create pictures in the reader's mind. | Make sure paragraphs are indented. |

Even if you teach kindergarten or 1st grade, students can still revise their writing with peers.

Once students draw, dictate, or write in response to a prompt, they should be encouraged to add details to it. This can be done using the following checklist, which is based on the six traits of writing, as a guide. The checklist includes some questions students could ask each other when working through the revision process.

| | Could you.... |
|---|---|
| Ideas | Add a drawing to help readers understand your writing? <br><br> Add descriptive words to help readers "see" what you are writing about? |
| Organization | Add a title? <br><br> Add transitions like *first, next, last*? |
| Word choice | Add figurative language, such as a simile? <br><br> Add a new word you learned at school that you don't use all the time? |
| Sentence fluency | Add words to make some sentences longer? Remember, not all sentences should be the same length. |
| Voice | Add oversize letters, exclamation points, underlining, repetition, and pictures for emphasis? |
| Language conventions | Add capital letters and periods at the end of sentences? |

Once students understand what they can add to their writing, you can provide some UDL choices to increase engagement in the revision process. Here are some examples:

- Take the class outside to write one or several sentences in chalk and then revise to improve.

- Allow groups of students to revise a piece together.

- Have students return to a previous drawing or writing piece to revise, using different colored pencils for each trait when they add something new.

## Publishing

Once students have drafted, revised, and edited their essays, they are ready to publish them, or turn them in, to receive a grade. Writing is a process, so you may find that students are much more successful when only their final product is assessed. Once you finish the process, students will have had multiple opportunities to gain mastery-oriented feedback; they will have had the process of writing broken down into manageable steps, which allows them to cope with the complicated task, and they have seen exemplars and been given a rubric, so they understand what success looks like.

To conclude, if you expect students to write an essay or an extended response, it is beneficial to break up the task into steps and scaffold it for them. Critics of this approach may argue that writing can't be quantified and that there is not one format to follow. That's absolutely true. Great writers don't need the scaffolding, but to become great writers, students need to learn about the writing process and they need to follow a format as a starting place. As you learned previously, great chefs don't follow recipes, but that's only because they have a recipe in mind. You may be able to make a cake from scratch, but it is because you have followed so many cake recipes, you know the necessary ingredients. Once you memorize those recipes, you can play with them, and the same is true for writing.

Your students who don't need the format won't use it, but make it available to everyone at the beginning of the year. Eventually, all students will be able to write with a greater level of independence, but they need help to get there.

## SUMMARY

When teaching a specific task or method, it's imperative to break up the task so all students can be successful. Reading and writing are learned skills, and both are built on the skeleton of literacy. Make that structure obvious to students who don't know it inherently. Doing this allows all students to access academic rigor. It's not up to us as teachers to decide which students will be successful. All students should have the opportunity to complete difficult tasks. The art of teaching is making those tasks reachable.

# DISCUSSION QUESTIONS

1. How much scaffolding do you do already in your learning environment? Are there any tasks that you assume students have background knowledge about and now you can see that scaffolding would be beneficial?

2. Why is it important for all teachers, across the content area, to model effective reading and writing strategies?

3. How can you implement more reading and writing instruction in your own learning environment?

# 9

# The Best Ways to Teach Vocabulary

About 10 years ago, I was at a party in Big Bear Lake, California. Over a plate of loaded nachos, I chatted with an acquaintance. At the end of the evening, while wiping his greasy fingers on a napkin, he thanked me for being so personable (at least that's where I think he was going). When he said, "It's been great talking to you. You are so personification," I didn't have the heart to correct him. If only one of his English teachers had taught him his literary terms, he wouldn't have looked . . . well, you know how it made him look.

Vocabulary is essential for students to succeed in reading, and a lack of vocabulary is often cited as one of the reasons why students

**Objective:** *You will be able to teach vocabulary using student-friendly, UDL-based strategies to improve vocabulary and reading comprehension.*

**Rationale:** By now you understand the need to give students different representations when teaching. One very important premise is that vocabulary should be taught in all subjects so students can learn essential content before having to utilize it. In this chapter, I will provide close to 20 ideas for helping students access new words and give other tips on how to represent information creatively.

lag behind in reading. When reading to learn, students must be able to define many unfamiliar, domain-specific words, and some children have a difficult time with this task. If students are not familiar with difficult vocabulary, they not only will have difficulty reading, but they will be disadvantaged on standardized achievement tests and in their future academic performance.

The best way to improve vocabulary? Read challenging text and get direct instruction on academic and domain-specific vocabulary. Vocabulary words can be characterized into three tiers. Tier 1 words are common words that are often used in oral language. Tier 2 words are general academic words that are useful in comprehending academic texts across disciplines. Words like *analyze, justify*, and *synthesize* are Tier 2 words. Tier 3 words are domain-specific words that students need to comprehend rigorous text in a particular content area—like the word *personification*.

A high volume of reading is imperative because fluency in reading is a function of practice in reading (Chall, 2000). Of course, reading must be scaffolded. Handing out books and expecting students to read independently without any instruction isn't the best way to increase comprehension or vocabulary.

All teachers, in all subject areas, need students to acquire new vocabulary. No longer, however, can we rely on the good old "drill and kill" method that was so popular when we were students. For some students, new vocabulary is simply not accessible when worksheets of vocabulary words and definitions are distributed. Because students' responses to vocabulary vary so greatly, we as teachers must present this vocabulary in different ways. In the Representation Guidelines, one checkpoint is "Clarify vocabulary and symbols." How we clarify new terms makes all the difference in whether students internalize and own the new words.

First, we need to teach students strategies for learning vocabulary. One of the ultimate goals of UDL is to teach students how to learn. In the UDL framework, teachers not only provide students with curriculum content but scaffold and model strategies so students can transfer skills and knowledge to other learning environments.

As a first step, all students should be taught how to use context clues to determine the meaning of unfamiliar words. In order to determine the meaning of unfamiliar words, students must understand the different types of context clues and how to use them. They must understand that the context is the words and sentences that surround the new word. Oftentimes, when reading, students will skip over unfamiliar words instead of trying to determine their meaning. As a publication for the International Reading Association noted nearly 30 years ago, "Don't assume that students know how to apply context clues when attacking unknown words; they have to be carefully taught" (Fuqua, 1985). This can begin as early as kindergarten and is still true today. The article outlines seven effective strategies for teaching context clues, which are aligned to the principles of UDL so they are tried and true and still used today.

1.  Picture clues

2.  Fill in the blank

3.  Listening

4.  Game playing

5.  Expanded reading

6.  Cloze procedure

7.  Teaching idioms

When teaching vocabulary, it's all about helping students recognize the meaning of words, which is necessary to activate their recognition networks (Figure 9-1).

## Universal Design for Learning Guidelines

| Affective Networks | Strategic Networks | Recognition Networks |
| --- | --- | --- |
| The "why" of learning | The "how" of learning | The "what" of learning |

| | | |
| --- | --- | --- |
| How learners get engaged and stay motivated. How they are challenged, excited, or interested. These are affective dimensions. | Planning and performing tasks. How we organize and express our ideas. Writing an essay or solving a math problem are strategic tasks. | How we gather facts and categorize what we see, hear, and read. Identifying letters, words, or an author's style are recognition tasks. |
| ☑ Stimulate interest and motivation for learning | ☑ Differentiate the ways students can express what they know | ☑ Present information and content in different ways |

**FIGURE 9-1:** Context Strategies to Activate Recognition Networks

The strategies are outlined in detail next.

As early as kindergarten, students can be taught about *picture clues.* If you display images of unfamiliar words, it can help students predict the definition and it also gives them a visual image. Although students may have an idea about certain words, a picture helps to solidify that image for them. For example, in a 7th-grade English class, when reading *The Jungle Books* by Rudyard Kipling, students used context clues to infer that Tarbarqui, the jackal, was some kind of animal, but they didn't know what type of animal he was. In the dictionary, a jackal is defined as any of several small omnivorous canids (as *Canis aureus*) of Africa and Asia having large ears, long legs, and bushy tails. This didn't help the students at all because they couldn't visualize him. After seeing the picture, however, they realized a jackal is similar to a coyote.

This allowed them to note characteristics of the jackal, and it helped them to characterize Tarbarqui later in the story as he fit in with what they already knew about coyotes. When displaying images to students, you can use Google Images, a PowerPoint, or another multimedia tool.

Also encourage students to do this on their own when they come to an unfamiliar word. The idiom "A picture speaks a thousand words" is so true in vocabulary.

In addition to using picture clues, you can teach students to *fill in the blanks* when they come to unfamiliar words. This is often the strategy that teachers think of when they think about context clues, as the words surrounding an unfamiliar word often help a reader to infer meaning.

You can teach students this strategy by scaffolding the fill-in-the-blank process. First, you can provide students with a list of domain-specific sentences with the unfamiliar words missing. Have them work together to determine the best missing word and have them discuss their strategies. You can model this by demonstrating the type of thinking you use when using this strategy. Once students are familiar with how to fill in the blanks, you can release more responsibility to them and provide them with sentences that include unfamiliar vocabulary words.

*Listening* is another way to practice filling in the blanks and is a great option for auditory learners. Practice reading paragraphs out loud and then pause, allowing students to guess the next word. In elementary school, rhyming books help students to learn this strategy, but it can be used with older students, as well. If students listen closely and carefully, they can often predict the next word in a sentence. In the true spirit of UDL, you can combine fill in the blank with the listening strategy so students can choose the representation that helps them to learn. If your students are more successful at listening for the missing word, you can encourage them to read the text out loud to themselves.

The next strategy is *game playing*. I don't know about you, but whenever I go to friends' houses and see word magnets on the refrigerator, I want to start making sentences. The same is true for students. In order to really own vocabulary words, students need to see them multiple times. Allowing students to play with words makes them fun. It's even better if you can encourage students to make the games themselves.

*Expanded reading* combines providing options for language and providing options for comprehension. It involves clarifying vocabulary by activating prior knowledge about a topic. Before reading, you can set a purpose and ask students to recall information they already know about a topic. For example, if you are about to read about volcanic eruption, ask the class to brainstorm difficult vocabulary that will probably be in the text. If students can predict the type of domain-specific words they will come across, they will be more likely to clue-in to the meaning of words.

Another strategy is the *cloze procedure*, which takes fill in the blank a step further. When using the cloze procedure, you delete words from a passage according to word count. For example, you may delete every 10th word and ask students to insert words as they read and construct meaning from the text, even with words missing. This is an especially good technique for note-taking. Instead of asking students to take notes for a whole period, provide them with "slotted notes" so they can fill in missing words as you are presenting information (using multiple means of representation, of course!).

Lastly, it's important to *clarify idioms* and other examples of figurative language. This is particularly important to promote understanding of vocabulary across languages. When learning reading comprehension strategies, it is valuable for students to learn that language is not only taken literally. Sometimes, when you're reading, you'll come across a familiar word but it may be used in an unfamiliar way. Students need to understand that words have multiple meanings, both literal and figurative, and so clues around the word are better indicators of a word's meaning than a dictionary definition. Provide examples of this for students so they can see how one word can mean very different things.

Another method for teaching vocabulary is robust vocabulary instruction (RVI), which "involves directly explaining the meaning of words in student friendly language and then following up with word play and scaffolded writing opportunities" (Beach et al., 2015). RVI is a five-step process that aligns closely to UDL.

**TABLE 9-1:** RVI Aligned to UDL (Adapted from Beach et al., 2015, p. 37)

| STEPS FOR TEACHING ACADEMIC VOCABULARY | ALIGNMENT TO UDL |
|---|---|
| 1. Select four Tier 2 words to teach each week. | |
| 2. Introduce words. Provide student-friendly explanations, definitions, and synonyms for each word. | Clarify vocabulary and symbols and support decoding of text by providing students with accessible definitions and images so they have a baseline understanding of the words. |
| 3. Facilitate discussion of the meaning of each word in illustrative instructional and authentic contexts. | Optimize relevance, value, and authenticity by giving students examples of how the word applies in their own lives. |
| 4. Engage students in word play. | Build fluencies with graduated levels of support for practice by creating prompts that encourage meaningful word play. |
| 5. Provide scaffolded writing opportunities. | Once students understand the meaning of the word, maximize transfer and generalization by asking them to apply the word in academic writing. |

The RVI process fosters critical thinking, because students have to apply the word in authentic contexts, engage in collaborative word play, and then use the word in writing. In a research study that examined the effectiveness of RVI on students with learning disabilities, a history teacher used word play with the word *acquire*. He prompted the students with the following: "I am going to say some words. If I say something that you would like to acquire, say 'acquire.' If not, say 'not acquire:' a bag of candy, a mosquito bite popularity, trust for your enemy" (Beach et al., 2015). After this activity, students discussed the nuanced meaning of the word as they reflected on their answers, and then used the newly acquired vocabulary word in their writing.

This writing can be scaffolded based on the needs of your students. The following list (from Beach et. al, 2015, p. 43) provides options for providing graduated levels of support for students.

1.  Substitute target words for synonym words or phrases.

2.  Complete cloze sentences using the most appropriate target word given the context.

3.  Complete sentence stems by selecting endings from multiple choices.

4.  Generate endings to sentence stems.

5.  Generate whole sentences without scaffolding.

Another option for scaffolding is that you can begin to use RVI as a class, and then encourage students to create groups and ask them to select their own Tier 2 or Tier 3 words and work through the process on their own, or facilitate the process for the rest of the class. This would allow students to create opportunities for their classmates to use challenging academic and domain-specific vocabulary in a collaborative and engaging environment and would help them practice their positive teamwork behaviors.

Context clues and RVI can help students to figure out the meaning of words, but as teachers, we want them to own the words. This requires students to see unfamiliar words repeatedly until they become familiar. What follows are some ideas you may want to implement in your classroom to help you do that. You can use them as routines, or you can change them up.

## THE WORD WALL

Make a Word Wall—that is, a bulletin board with all the vocabulary words presented throughout the year. You can put students in charge of creating and updating this wall, but the simple act of seeing the words repeatedly will allow students to use them more often. When students use the words in a variety of contexts, they are more likely to own them. At the beginning of the year, you could start a countdown. For example, you may want to introduce 200 words during the year. Students love watching the countdown progress as they learn more words.

I once observed a class where a Word Wall was used. Each day, the teacher used the board as an activator he called "Word Wizard." During this activity, it was a student's responsibility to write clever sentences using any of the vocabulary words on the wall. Some of the words were *cynical, threat, retaliate,* and *eloquent.* During the five-minute activity, students had to create different sentences very quickly and then share them with the class. He used this *game playing* technique to help students use the words in different ways.

The class appeared genuinely excited to complete this activity. When one student offered, "Even though the president gave an eloquent speech, the nation was still cynical," a girl in the back of the room clapped her hands loudly and stated, "Oh—that's hot!" The teacher did not allow any misuse of vocabulary to slide. For example, a student offered the sentence, "The hero made an eloquent threat and retaliation." He replied, "Nope. That's not right. You're trying to use too many words. Pick one and use it correctly. That is more important to be able to do." Although the answer seemed harsh, the student went right back to work and raised his hand again later. His next sentence was correct. Clearly, the teacher was a warm demander and created a culture where mastery-oriented feedback was the norm. What a great way to incorporate vocabulary instruction daily.

## VOCABULARY JAR

Another fun way to add on to the Word Wall is to have a vocabulary jar. On your desk, place a large glass jar. Every time a student uses a prior vocabulary word correctly, either in writing or orally, they can write the word and its definition on a raffle ticket and put it in the jar. The more vocabulary they use and recognize, the more chances they will have at winning. Once a week or when the jar is full, you can pull a ticket and the student wins a prize, like a homework pass, candy, or classroom supplies. Regardless of how you decide to use the jar or the Word Wall, it communicates a message to students that words are not meant to be memorized and forgotten. We must use our words to own them. If you are worried about students interrupting class to get tickets, you can just have students come up at the end of class to get their tickets.

## WORD WORK

Set up a routine that allows students to participate in word work, where they study common affixes and word relationships, such as synonyms and antonyms, to help them analyze words when context is lacking. When students have explicit instruction in word parts, word relationships, and word origins, they are more likely to use their word knowledge to figure out the meaning of unfamiliar words. You could teach prefixes or word roots and include them on the Word Wall. Challenge students to see how many words they can find that use the "affix of the week."

## THE FRAYER MODEL

If you have a really important concept that students need to learn, you could have them create concept maps for the word. One popular method is the Frayer Model, which encourages students to think critically about definitions to determine characteristics, non-critical characteristics, examples, and non-examples. You could ask students to present their models to peers so they are speaking about the unfamiliar word. This is especially important for Tier 2 and Tier 3 words because they are frequently seen only in text.

Although this is a great activity, completing the chart takes time, so pick out the most important ones and ask students to complete the chart. They could even re-create the graphic in their notebooks so you don't have to make copies.

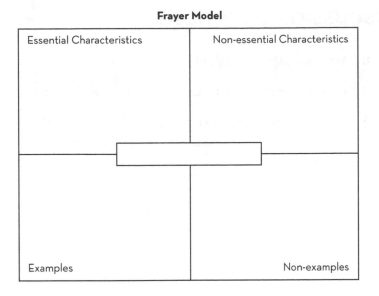

**Frayer Model**

| Essential Characteristics | Non-essential Characteristics |
|---|---|
| | |
| Examples | Non-examples |

Regardless of how you want to encourage reading, teach context clues, or review vocabulary, it's helpful to keep the UDL Guidelines in mind. Even if you're not a reading or English teacher, we all are teachers of literacy, and we have a responsibility not only to teach our content but to teach our students how to access our content. Ideally some of the vocabulary strategies in this chapter will help you to do that.

## SUMMARY

It is imperative that all teachers clarify vocabulary and symbols in order for student critical thinking ability and reading comprehension to improve. In order to own new vocabulary, students need repeated exposure to the words and authentic opportunities to use the words in writing and in text to increase their value. Asking students to memorize words does not increase their understanding of complex topics, nor does it contribute to increased scores on standardized tests. In order for students to increase their vocabulary, they must read challenging text, learn how to use context clues, and continue to use the words throughout the school year.

# DISCUSSION QUESTIONS

1.  What are all the benefits of students increasing their vocabulary?

2.  How do you currently teach vocabulary to your students?

3.  Are there any strategies in this chapter that you could implement immediately to help students increase their vocabulary in your subject area?

# Using Student Feedback to Inform Instruction

# 10

Practice makes perfect, right? That's certainly true when it comes to cooking. When I first started making my own homemade pizza dough, I was pretty darn proud of myself. I had a fancy bread machine that could whip up a batch of whole-wheat dough while I sat outside and read about how to make it from scratch in *Food Network Magazine*. It didn't get better than that pizza dough . . . until my sister came over with a bag of multigrain dough from Whole Foods. I argued that I had already slaved over my own dough, but sissy assured me that her selection would pair better with the roasted butternut squash topping. We then did what any sisters would do. We had a bake-off. Unfortunately,

**Objective:** *Teachers will learn to provide rich, mastery-oriented feedback to students but also to provide them with opportunities to give the teachers feedback that improves instruction.*

**Rationale:** In order to improve practice, professionals need feedback. Asking students to contribute feedback is an excellent opportunity to reflect on your teaching methods and improve UDL instruction.

the heartiness and the crunch of the Whole Foods pizza crust made me reevaluate my recipe.

After everyone at the table agreed that my own crust paled in comparison to the multigrain version, I started to seek feedback. What exactly was so good about the crust? Was it the texture? The salt content? I needed specifics.

That started my yearlong goal of replicating that Whole Foods dough. Every time I made a new batch, I needed guidance. I asked my husband, "Is this better than the last one?" When he wanted to indulge me, he'd make some comment like, "I think you used too much flax in this one. It's stuck in my teeth." A problem identified is a problem soon to be fixed.

I wish I could tell you that my pizza dough is now interchangeable with the delicious Whole Foods version, but it's not. Yet. The thing is, I'm a heck of a lot closer than when I started because of the feedback. It's made me a better cook. The same concept will make you a better teacher. Shaping kids' minds is somewhat like shaping dough. It takes a lot of practice. Regardless of where you're teaching and how much good work you're doing with kids, you always know that somewhere out there, someone is doing it better. Instead of denying it, work to become better at what you do.

Teaching is a very private profession. The only time we get feedback is when it's on an evaluation—and then, it's often an assessment, not an opportunity to reflect, rethink, and reteach. Administrators are busy. As much as they'd like to come into classrooms and give us the feedback we crave, there is not a lot of time. Students offer a powerful and immediate source of feedback—if you're ready to listen to them. Whatever knowledge you're cooking up in your learning environment, the kids are the ones eating it. Every decision we make in the classroom affects them and their future. We have an obligation to teach them and to serve them. To do that well, we need their feedback.

One great informal way to collect feedback is to interview students. Once you have questions you would like to ask, survey students or interview specific students who need to know that you care about their opinion. You will probably want to know what students are thinking and how they view your educational environment before they share those opinions with evaluators. This gives you a chance to make changes and improve your instruction. Think of student feedback as a formative assessment. Their mastery-oriented feedback can help you become a better teacher so you can excel on your summative evaluation.

When surveying students to collect feedback, you have a couple of options. You can collect feedback informally, collect it formally, or use a combination of both methods. If you choose to collect informal feedback, you can ask students questions like the following: What assignments help you to feel the most successful? Which assignments or activities are frustrating to you and why? How will my assignments help you in other classes, in future grades, or in life?

The answers to these questions may be hard to hear, but they will provide you with valuable feedback about the ways that students view you and your classroom, and this will allow you to know them a little better. The better you know the students, the easier it is to make assignments and lessons that are interesting and relevant to them.

Having an archive of student voice is valuable, because without it, there is nothing concrete to ground your reflection. You can't assume you know what students are thinking. You need their voices. Once you have their feedback, you can't deny proof that is right in front of you. When you reassess your UDL practice, it's not about being critical of yourself. It's about responding to a specific student comment. Ask yourself, "What could I do in class so this student feels more supported?" or something similar. Once you decide on a course of action, you can implement it and then check back in with the student. This sends a powerful message that you are working to teach each individual student and that you don't have a one-size-fits-all approach to education.

Another way to collect student feedback informally is to add a couple of questions at the end of each assignment or assessment. The simple questions "How did you feel about this test? Did you feel prepared for it? Why or why not?" will provide you with valuable feedback about instruction. You could also ask students to predict their grades on the test and outline reasons why they performed the way they did. This will also help you to make important instructional decisions.

After teaching each standard, ask students to grade their knowledge of the standard on a scale of A–F. This strategy was outlined in Chapter 4, but appears below, as well.

*Give yourself a grade for your understanding of each standard based on today's lesson.*

| | A | B | C | D | F |
|---|---|---|---|---|---|
| Interpret differences in shape, center, and spread in the context of the data sets, accounting for possible effects of extreme data points (outliers). | | | | | |
| Represent data on two quantitative variables on a scatter plot, and describe how the variables are related. | | | | | |

When you are finished, answer one of the following questions:

1. Did the lesson help you to meet the standards? If not, what was confusing about the lesson?

2. What could you have done better today?

3. What could I, as your teacher, have done better today?

4. Did you enjoy today's lesson? Why or why not?

In addition to asking students about your practice informally, you can also use a validated survey, such as the Tripod survey, which measures student perception about the 7 Cs (Ferguson, 2012), all of which relate to UDL Guidelines. Table 10-1 explains each of the 7 Cs and how they relate to the UDL principles. Even if you have no intention of purchasing the survey, it's interesting to learn about the 7 Cs and how you can incorporate them into your learning environment.

**TABLE 10-1:** The 7 Cs and How They Relate to UDL

| | |
|---|---|
| **Care:** Teachers help students feel safe and welcome. | • Minimize threats and distractions. |
| **Control:** Teacher has effective classroom management and allows students to spend appropriate time on-task. | • Facilitate managing information and resources.<br>• Minimize threats and distractions. |
| **Clarify:** Teacher promotes understanding and helps students to persevere. | • Provide options for language, mathematical expressions, and symbols.<br>• Build fluencies with graduated levels of support for practice and performance.<br>• Guide appropriate goal-setting.<br>• Support planning and strategy development.<br>• Enhance capacity for monitoring progress.<br>• Promote expectations and beliefs that optimize motivation.<br>• Facilitate personal coping skills and strategies. |
| **Challenge:** Teacher creates curriculum that both is rigorous and requires student effort. | • Vary demands and resources to optimize challenge. |
| **Captivate:** Teachers make lessons engaging and stimulating. | • Vary the methods for response and navigation.<br>• Optimize individual choice and autonomy.<br>• Optimize relevance, value, and authenticity. |
| **Confer:** Students are invited to participate in class, express themselves, and work together. | • Foster collaboration and community.<br>• Develop self-assessment and reflection. |
| **Consolidate:** Teacher frequently checks for understanding and organizes materials to help students remember important content. | • Highlight patterns, critical features, big ideas, and relationships.<br>• Support planning and strategy development.<br>• Increase mastery-oriented feedback. |

Using a validated survey may help you to gain valuable, systematic feedback. For more information on the Tripod project, visit their website at http://tripodproject.org.

## THE CONNECTION BETWEEN STUDENT FEEDBACK AND BEGINNING-OF-THE-YEAR SURVEYS

Whether you decide to collect feedback informally or formally, students need to know that you take their perspectives seriously. You will get much more valuable feedback if you start listening to their voices early in the year. An excellent way to set the tone at the beginning of the year is to distribute student surveys. The surveys should allow you to learn personal information about students that you would not learn otherwise. You can hand out a paper survey, set up a link for an online survey, or ask students to express their answers in an interview setting. Either way, it's valuable to get to know your students.

When you are surveying students, you may want to start with simple questions about their interests, such as the following:

- What do you like to do with your friends?

- Do you play on any teams? If so, which ones?

- Who is your role model and why?

- What is your favorite movie? Sports team? Food?

- What are your goals for five years from now? Ten years from now? Don't feel as though you have to be realistic. Dream big and sometimes big things happen.

Once you collect the information, use it in class to engage students. If some of your students love baseball, bring in box scores for graphing, newspaper articles for summarizing, or game clips for editing as choice assignments. If some your students love chocolate, have them write an argument on the best chocolate bar. In short, use their interests to get them interested in learning. Also, you can connect with students on a personal level, which makes them feel like they are valued in the learning community.

In addition to learning about students, you can dig deeper and find out about the way they view the world. For example, you may ask the following:

- What, in your opinion, is the happiest kind of life for a human being?

- How would you describe a good person?

- What would make you truly happy in your life? Think about what you really want when you grow older.

- What is your definition of work ethic?

- What is your definition of courage?

Once you are familiar with students' interests and the way they view the world and define a successful future, you can assist them in seeing the connections between school and life, which will help you to make learning relevant. Tell them that writing a business letter will help them get funding for the skateboard park they are dreaming about. Tell them that using argument will help them get a raise at their job so they will be able to buy their dream house. Students need to understand that learning can help them. Teaching needs to be personal. It only takes a minute to go around the room and give an example that is personalized for each student.

Once you understand the variability in students' interests and how they view the world, you can differentiate processes by providing varying learning activities when you design your lessons. It's not up to you to choose how the students learn. It's up to you to provide options they will want to choose to learn. If you don't know your students, you can't design a curriculum that is relevant to them.

On the student survey, you could also include a section about personal coping strategies so you can plan lessons that help all students access your material. In this section, you could ask such questions as the following:

- If you don't know the meaning of a word you come across when reading or listening to someone talk, what do you do?

- What is the most enjoyable school assignment you have ever completed? Why?

- If you had to learn about any five topics (that are school appropriate, of course), what would they be?

- What was the most memorable lesson a teacher has ever presented to you? Why was it so memorable?

- What type of assignments do you have trouble with? What about those assignments creates an obstacle for you?

- What helps you to learn the best in school? When you're with your friends? When you're at home?

- Do you feel safe in school? Why or why not? Do you feel safe in this classroom? Why or why not?

Taking the time to get to know students helps them to realize you care about them as learners. The next step is to ask for their feedback to help design lessons that challenge and engage them. Then, check in with students early and often to collect valuable feedback about how you are doing so you can improve your own instruction throughout the year. As stated previously, there are countless ways to collect data, so choose the option that works best for you and your students. That's what UDL is all about!

## SUMMARY

Bringing student voices into the learning environment is an invaluable way to reflect and evaluate your practice. In order to get the most honest, mastery-oriented feedback, students need to know you care about them and their perspectives, so start at the beginning of the year weaving their voices into your practice. If they know they are valued, they will be much more willing to give you specific, concrete feedback that will make you a better teacher, while also making them better students.

# DISCUSSION QUESTIONS

1. Student feedback is beginning to be incorporated into many teacher evaluation tools. How do you feel about that?

2. How do you currently collect feedback from students to inform your instruction?

3. Are you more comfortable with collecting student feedback in formal or informal ways? Which ideas from the chapter will you implement immediately?

4. How is the practice of learning about students related to the quality of their feedback later in the year?

# 11

# Assessments the UDL Way

## (Yes, Standardized Assessments, Too!)

As we are all well aware, there is a significant test-score gap between the country's lowest and highest students. Clearly, every district in the country is making an attempt to educate all students so they have equal opportunities for achievement, but even with supportive legislation and money, the gap is still present. Critics of education note that the gap is due in part to teacher expectations. This line of reasoning suggests that if teachers are part of the problem, they are also part of the solution.

This belief fires up every teacher in America, with good reason. But maybe we shouldn't be so quick to attack critics. Are they wrong? Yes, but they may have a point. We do have the power to increase student

**Objective:** *You will learn that preparing students for standardized tests is not the same as "teaching to the test." Also, UDL strategies can help you to prepare your students to perform to the best of their ability.*

**Rationale:** Standardized tests are here to stay, so regardless of how you feel about them, you need to prepare your students for the test-taking challenge. This chapter outlines ideas to support student planning and strategy development for success on these objective measures.

achievement. Alone, we cannot close the gap, but we are brilliant and dedicated and we have the power to change kids' lives. Instead of fighting with critics, we should put our passion to better use—doing everything we can to prove them wrong. One way to do this is to take the time to prepare students to take the tests that are so important for them.

The limitations of standardized achievement tests aside, for students who are at risk of failing, a challenging curriculum is crucial for success on these tests. This is not to say that any teacher should "teach to the test." Instead, teachers should focus on standards and actively involve students in learning.

As we all know, standardized tests are a reality, and although they may not be universally designed, they are aligned to the standards we are required to teach. If we teach a universally designed curriculum embedding next-generation skills, our students will be self-directed, motivated learners, creative and practical problem-solvers, and critical thinkers who have an understanding of the knowledge and skills we have taught them. These students will perform well, even if the tests have barriers. As Jon Mundorf, a UDL legend, says, "I would rather teach in an accessible way to an inaccessible test, than in an inaccessible way for an inaccessible test." Knowing this, you don't have to "teach to the test" throughout the year.

With the cloud of standardized tests looming above us like a bad storm, teachers struggle with whether or not choice is appropriate on formative or summative assessments in their own classrooms. So let's dive into the true meaning of the different types of assessments so that you can consider how choice is always valuable in your practice.

To begin, any assessment that informs instruction is super valuable, and these are often administered before teaching a unit of instruction. Sometimes these assessments are called *diagnostic assessments*, and other times they are called *formative assessments*, but the purpose is the same. When these assessments are given, teachers use the data or results to inform instruction, based on their new awareness of students' strengths and areas of weakness. Giving students a choice assignment before planning instruction increases engagement, removes barriers, and also allows students to practice self-direction and creativity as they share what they know (also, these assessments are way more fun to correct!).

Once students have learned material, through access to a universally designed curriculum, teachers can give *summative assessments*, which measure a student's growth since the formative assessment. Both formative and summative assessment can take many different shapes. As long as the product allows teachers to assess student learning in response to specific standards, the assessment is doing its job. It's okay if these summative assessments do not take traditional forms. You can assess students' knowledge in a choice assessment, even while preparing for standardized exams.

You do not need to sacrifice yearlong quality instruction for student success on standardized tests, but you need to do just a little preparation for the tests immediately before the test administration to put students' mind at ease. It's the same principle as when we, as adults, get medical procedures.

Before getting a diagnostic medical procedure, you have a pre-op appointment (think mammogram, colonoscopy, bone marrow test, and so forth). During this appointment, your doctor tells you exactly what to expect before, during, and after your procedure. Your doctor will explain the exact preparations you have to make, such as fasting, drinking 15 gallons of sickly sweet orange cleansing tonic, and/or removing jewelry; explain how long the procedure will take; and explain what to expect as an outcome. This pre-op appointment allows you to feel more in control from the moment you walk into the hospital until the moment you are discharged. You have ample opportunities to ask questions and have your concerns heard. Before going through a procedure, the doctor or nurse walks you through it so you know exactly what to expect. The same philosophy needs to be true for standardized tests.

For many students, sitting down for hours to take a standardized test is like a painful medical procedure. If you're a strong tester, this may seem ridiculous, but just accept that, for some students, taking a standardized test is like drilling into their femur. If you can accept this as truth, it will allow you to make preparations accordingly. Remember, UDL is about universally designing lessons. Your test-prep curriculum needs to account for the students you may have who are anxious about the test or couldn't care less. How can you engage students, motivate them, and prepare them? That's where your craft comes in.

Just like a surgery, your students need to be prepared for this procedure so they feel more comfortable and in control. In other words, students need specific scaffolding so they know how to succeed on these tests. They may not like it, but these tests are important for their long-term academic health. It's a national check-up of sorts. Granted, there are critics of standardized tests, but that doesn't change that fact that tests are a very real obstacle for students. You can hope that the tests will go away, but that's unlikely. Even if departments of education pull back on standardized tests, students will still need to take these objective tests to enter college, enter the military, join the police academy, or even get their license. We, as teachers, cannot assume that students have the necessary skills to be successful on these tests. Teaching them the content and providing them with a next-generation education is a necessary first step, but that is not enough. They need to know how about the types of questions, how the tests are scored, and why performing well is important.

All of this can be done through successful scaffolding. I am in no way arguing that you teach to the test. But preparing students for a test is not teaching to the test. It's teaching a valuable skill, which is one of many important skills. This is not something you need to do all year. Throughout the year, you teach to your standards, and your formative and summative assessments measure progress on those standards. If you're teaching your standards, they will have the knowledge and skills necessary to take the test.

The question is, will they be able to transfer that knowledge to the test? To answer that question, teach standardized test-taking as a unit. Go into prep mode a couple of weeks before the test is to be administered. This allows students enough time to learn why they are taking the test, what the test measures, and how to be as successful as they can be. Think of this as their pre-op appointment. So, how do you do this?

First, before you prepare students for taking the test, make sure the students know why the test is administered and how the scores are used. There are always students who fail because they just guess or they don't take it seriously. You have to engage them and make it relevant to them. What happens if they score well? What happens if they don't? Answering these important questions relates back to the hidden curriculum. If this test is taking days out of their lives, they need to know why. It may feel scary to admit that it's in large part to measure teacher accountability, but they deserve to know that. Get the students to invest in you. You work hard all year to make sure they are learning the standards. You deserve to know how much they have grown. You need students to buy into this. Do what it takes to get the students to perform the best they can, but also, ease the pressure on them. I always tell students that the standardized tests are more about me than about them. I want to carry the stress for them so they can show off how brilliant they all are.

After they understand why they have to take the test, students need to see what the test looks like. If you have copies of previous tests, show these to students. Show them as many as you can. You can create stations where students explore the tests on their own or you can project passages and questions for students to see. While you project the tests, explain the different parts of the tests and what the goal of each section is. The goal of this step is to get students comfortable with the format of the test. How many questions will there be? How long will they have to take the test? As with any other new skill, don't assume the students have prior knowledge. Even if you're teaching high school, students may not have seen what the SAT looks like. Make them comfortable with the format so there are no surprises there. It's like teaching the basics of a recipe to a new chef. You don't know what the ingredients will be every time, but you know that a recipe always follows the same formula.

Second, model test-taking strategies as you answer questions. Multiple-choice questions are tricky especially now since many of the standardized tests include "hot spots" or the option to select more than one correct answer. If there were only one obvious answer, every student would get it right. Students need to know that multiple-choice questions use tricks that distract students from correct answers. These same strategies are at work whether you teach 3rd grade or AP classes. Point them out to students so they have power when they go into take the tests. I tell them, "Those test takers will try to trick you, but they won't know that you'll get the best of them." Make them feel like they are in cahoots with you.

If students are taking the test online, familiarize yourself with the skills students will need to be successful in that environment. These skills can be broken down into three categories: keyboarding skills, mouse or track-pad skills, and general online assessment skills.

The Office of Special Education Programs, U.S. Department of Education, awarded the University of Kentucky, in collaboration with CAST, a directed research project grant titled Universal Design of Assessment: Applications of Technology. One of the research activities in this project was to identify the prerequisite skills for students to successfully access and use a computer-based assessment. Table 11-1 outlines those skills, for your review.

**TABLE 11-1:** Online Assessment Skill Breakdown

| SKILLS | BREAKDOWN OF SKILLS |
|---|---|
| Keyboarding skills | • Identify, locate, and use letter, number, and punctuation keys to enter characters<br>• Use enter/return key<br>• Use space bar<br>• Use delete key<br>• Use backspace key<br>• Use shift key<br>• Use tab key<br>• Use number pad<br>• Use keyboard to type letters and numerals<br>• Enter characters with reasonable accuracy (i.e., 85%)<br>• Enter characters with reasonable speed |
| Mouse or track-pad skills | • Use single-click function of the mouse<br>• Use double-click function of the mouse<br>• Use click-and-drag function of the mouse. This is important for drag-and-drop questions.<br>• Use a mouse to highlight text on a screen |

**TABLE 11-1:** Online assessment skill breakdown  *CONTINUED*

| SKILLS | BREAKDOWN OF SKILLS |
|---|---|
| Online assessment skills (general) | • Scroll to view complete text or question<br><br>• Scroll to navigate to a response section<br><br>• Scroll within each box of a split screen<br><br>• Toggle between tabs in a split screen<br><br>• Enter text by typing directly into expandable text response box<br><br>• Using an onscreen video player<br><br>• Use hot-spot zones: unlike a traditional multiple-choice item where only one answer option can be selected, hot-spot items may require the student to select one or more hot-spot zones (answer options) in order to correctly answer the item<br><br>• Online calculator, equation editor, ruler, and protractor |

Once students know the necessary skills to be successful on the test, the format of the test and strategies for answering questions, show them exemplary work. Many states post student work samples to analyze. Post the most stellar examples of short answers, open responses, and essays for students to read. Show them as many as you can. Students can work in groups to highlight essays and break them down into the different traits of writing or can make presentations on why the answers are so strong. This practice models the best work. You may be hesitant to show struggling students the best work, for fear of making them feel like they won't measure up, but think of it another way. If students never see exceptional work, they will never be able to create it. Do not water down student samples because that is lowering the bar for your own students. They deserve to see what they are measured against. It's then your job to get them to measure up.

The night before the test, have a test "pep rally." Remind students to get a good night's sleep and eat breakfast. If you have students who don't have the resources, think back to the idea of removing barriers. If you have to bring in a box of granola bars, it's worth it. Provide pencils, highlighters, mints, or bottles of water. If your students need something to be successful on the test, provide it for them. Don't allow the lack of a breakfast to be an excuse for students.

Teaching students your standards is something that you will focus on all year, not because of a test but because that's your calling. Prepping for the actual test is a valuable activity to complete a week or two before the test. Don't focus yearlong instruction on the test. If you teach your students to think critically, they will be able to transfer their knowledge. You just need to make sure that they feel comfortable enough to do that.

## A QUICK NOTE ON TRADITIONAL TESTS

In addition to standardized tests, many teachers give frequent tests and quizzes to assess student knowledge of curriculum content. Clearly, traditional multiple-choice tests are not the most UDL-friendly assessments. Before giving an assessment, ask yourself if it would be possible to assign a choice assessment or scaffold a writing assignment where students can express their content knowledge and practice literacy skills. Those are always the best options, but sometimes, the correcting of such assignments can seem overwhelming and you just need to give a traditional assessment. Even if you do this, there are ways to prepare students to take these types of tests. Just remember to scaffold the process and prepare them to take that type of assessment, and they will be more likely to succeed.

## SUMMARY

Although it seems like UDL is incompatible with standardized testing, the Guidelines can actually help you prepare students to succeed on the test. Just make sure to follow the principles of scaffolding to give students an opportunity to experience the testing process in a safe environment. Using the strategies outlined in this chapter will help you to prepare students to show off their knowledge appropriately.

# DISCUSSION QUESTIONS

1.  How does your school currently view test preparation? Is it different from the philosophy outlined in this chapter? How so?

2.  After reading this chapter, can you explain how standardized test prep can align with the principles of scaffolded instruction?

3.  How can we use scaffolding before standardized tests to "raise the floor" and have all students lifted up; is it also possible to diminish or completely delete test anxiety in the classroom?

4.  In order for students to appreciate the importance of testing, you have to believe in its value, at least a little. Search yourself and identify some benefits to standardized testing.

# 12

# Technology Helps!

If you've ever seen the movie *Napoleon Dynamite*, you probably remember the closing scene where Kip pens a beautiful love song to his wife, Lafawnda. The heartfelt ballad contains the lyrics "I love technology, but not as much as you, you see. Yes, I love technology, always and forever." That's a sentiment shared by pretty much every person in the country, especially our students.

Although technology and UDL go hand in hand, UDL is really about a love for learning in general, regardless of the presence of such wonderful tools as iPads, laptops, Chromebooks, and Apple TVs. As you've learned in previous chapters, teachers can implement UDL using many low-tech strategies. You don't need the newest and best equipment to create choice assessments, scaffold instruction, or

**Objective:** *You will learn about all the resources in the online component of this book and will learn how to incorporate some cool technologies into your UDL-based learning environment.*

**Rationale:** UDL is not only about technology, but there are some awesome resources that can enrich UDL lessons.

engage students. That being said, technology certainly doesn't hurt and can actually make UDL implementation much easier. Although technology is important, I waited until the end of the book to address it because it's good to know that you can still teach without it.

## REPRESENTATION AND TECHNOLOGY

So, how can you use technology to make your UDL lessons even better? Let's return to the three networks and discuss all the tools that relate to each network. First, when representing information to students, technology allows you to easily customize the display of information. When you hand out written text, the text is confined to the page. Students can't make it bigger or smaller or change the color of the text. The paper can't read the text to them, and even if you're lucky enough to have a color printer, students can't interact with the images. A computer makes all of this possible. When you create handouts on the computer, students can download files to tablets, phones, or a classroom computer. Students then have the choice to customize the text to their preference.

Text-to-speech software is also beneficial for students. This software allows students to click on text and have it read aloud to them. If you have a computer lab, students can wear headphones and listen to text at their own pace.

The National UDL Center also has additional tools that allow you to provide options for perception. One fantastic tool is called CAST UDL Book Builder (http://bookbuilder.cast.org). UDL Book Builder allows you to create modified texts by enriching the text with audio cues, discussion questions, and visuals. In your book, you can highlight patterns, critical features, and big ideas, and you can clarify vocabulary and symbols. By integrating the text with guided, scaffolded reading strategies, students can use technology to increase their reading comprehension strategies.

If you have a class projector or Apple TV, it's much easier to create presentations that include video and audio components. PowerPoints and Prezis are presentations that you can embed both sound and images into. This allows student to perceive multiple modalities at one time. If you want to see an increase in engagement, take a handout that you used to give students in hard copy, and turn it into an electronic handout.

You can utilize free applications to make your presentations more accessible. I've highlighted some here, along with short descriptions. You can use all basic tools for free.

- Google Docs or Google Slides

- Prezi (https://prezi.com). Create fluid, non-linear presentations where you can zoom around the screen as you present content.

- Haiku Deck (www.haikudeck.com). A nice alternative to Power-Point, because it is easy to use, but creates more elegant, simple presentations.

- Powtoon (www.powtoon.com). Create animated videos and presentations.

- HapYak (http://corp.hapyak.com). Explore an amazing place you can use to post videos as resources. If you want your students to view a video, you can use the video annotation service to focus and assist your learners in the process of understanding the video. HapYak allows you to add annotations, divide the video into chapters, add links to supporting information, and create in-video assessments. HapYak allows for the creation of five interactive videos per month for free. Also note that you can use the transcription services of YouTube for videos under 10 minutes to provide a text version of your videos.

- MindMup (www.mindmup.com). Draw and create mind maps that are saved into your Google Drive to share with students.

- Animoto (https://animoto.com). Create short videos accompanied by music.

- ThingLink (www.thinglink.com). Add roll-over links to an image in an interactive video.

- Smore (www.smore.com). Beautiful electronic newsletter.

- FlipSnack (www.flipsnack.com). Make a presentation into a flip book.

- Voki (www.voki.com). Create a talking avatar.

## EXPRESSION AND TECHNOLOGY

If you have technology available, you can also provide many options for students to express their knowledge. Many assistive technologies, like joysticks and speech-recognition software, require the use of a computer. Also, students have the option of typing an assignment if a computer lab is available. A number of software programs assess students as they are working on the computer. These programs provide instant mastery-oriented feedback and provide tips for planning and strategy development. One such tool is Study Island (www.studyisland.com). The Study Island website claims to help "K–12 students master state-specific, grade-level academic standards in a fun and engaging manner." Study Island is one such product of its kind, but there are many others that will help you to engage students, while also aligning instruction to mandated standards.

Another amazing website is No Red Ink (www.noredink.com). This site allows teachers to create classroom logins so students can get unlimited help with writing and specific grammar skills. Modules are based on student interest, which makes it very UDL-friendly, and you can track growth throughout the year.

Students can also express knowledge using technology. Choice assessments can include endless options, including all technology outlined in the section "Representation and Technology." Give them options and be amazed at the results. Allowing choices beyond traditional paper and pencil assignments will surely get students more engaged.

## ENGAGEMENT AND TECHNOLOGY

Let's face it. Our students were born into technology. All the new technology that we struggle to learn about is as innate to them as breathing. When they go home at night, they are on Snapchat, Twitter, Instagram, and countless other networking sites we probably don't even know about yet. So, if you want to get their attention, it doesn't hurt to get on the grid.

In order to build coping skills when it comes to digital literacy, it's important that students know how to keyboard. Many of our students are proficient texters with their two thumbs but their words per minute (WPM) rates leave little to be desired. If you want to support your students as they build their keyboarding fluency, you can introduce them to a free typing site, like www.typeracer.com, which will improve their skills in no time.

## THE ONLINE COMPONENT

Technology is important not only to students but to educators, as well. Many teachers now use social networks to connect with like-minded educators from across the country. They even have virtual conferences. Because technology engages you, just as it engages your students, there is a website to supplement this text, www.katienovakudl.com.

The website contains numerous resources to implement UDL in your classroom. One important aspect of UDL is the ability to present information to learners in a way that they can customize the display of information. This is especially valuable when you want to customize assignments for your own learning environments. On the website, you can access assignments, templates, and rubrics, which are available for download in various formats. This makes it easy to download the documents and personalize them for your own students.

Also, for each chapter in this text, there is a multimedia presentation that outlines the most important information in the chapter and displays it visually. If you want to use this text in a PLC or in a district professional development setting, you're welcome to use the presentations, or revise them as needed.

There are so many fantastic opportunities to connect with like-minded educators on social media. In the spirit of UDL, you have numerous choices to connect with other readers. First, you can connect with me any time at www.katienovakudl.com or novak414@gmail.com. If you'd prefer, you can also connect with other UDL practitioners on Twitter. Twice a month, there is a chat at #udlchat, where educators share what they're doing with UDL, and you can always reach me at @KatieNovakUDL. You'll find all the information about social media on the webpage.

## SUMMARY

Throughout the text, you have learned about UDL and how you can begin to implement the UDL Guidelines into your practice. Even if you start slowly, the shift will be valuable for your students. The UDL approach puts student variability first and helps you to design lessons that will never need to be modified or changed to accommodate differing levels of learners. Given that the country is moving toward college- and career-ready standards, all teachers are expected to prepare students to meet rigorous content standards, and UDL will help you to do this. Return to this text often as a reminder of all the small ways you can make a big difference in your practice.

In closing, keep the Guidelines close, align instruction to the standards, and empower students by embracing their voice. Lastly, have fun. Learning should be engaging and stimulating for all learners, and it can't possibly be enjoyable for them if it's not enjoyable to you. You chose a job where you can make a difference in the lives of children and in the future of our nation. What an honor. Never forget that.

As stated in the introduction to this book, your decision to implement UDL reflects a mind-set, a core belief that your students are capable of higher-order critical thinking, literacy, and true understanding of your content. The goal of UDL is not for students to get good grades; it's for students to learn and, in that process, learn how to learn. This way, the lessons of UDL will be with them always. They will be expert learners today and successful adults in years to come.

# DISCUSSION QUESTIONS

1. How can the concept of UDL change your teaching?

2. In regards to UDL, what are your strengths as a teacher or administrator?

3. In regards to UDL, what teaching or leadership skills do you need to continue working on?

4. What aspects of UDL will be the easiest to implement? What will be the most challenging?

5. If someone asked you about Universal Design for Learning, what would you say?

# A

# UDL Resources

Visit the National UDL Center at www.udlcenter.org and visit CAST at www.cast.org. For a comprehensive presentation on the UDL Guidelines, including research evidence, examples, and helpful implementation tools, go to www.udlcenter.org/aboutudl/udlguidelines. CAST provides a number of free learning resources and teacher tools based on UDL at www.cast.org/learningtools/.

To read more about UDL, the following books will help:

- Hall, T. E., Meyer, A., & Rose, D. H. (2012). *Universal design for learning in the classroom: Practical applications.* New York, NY: Guilford.

- Meyer, A., Rose, D. H., & Gordon, D. (2014). *Universal design for learning: Theory and practice.* Wakefield, MA: CAST Professional Publishing. Also published online at http://udltheorypractice .cast.org.

- Nelson, L. L. (2013). *Design and deliver: Planning and teaching using universal design for learning.* Baltimore, MD: Brookes.

See also:

- Gordon, D. T., Gravel, J. W., & Schifter, L. A. (2009). *A policy reader in universal design for learning.* Cambridge, MA: Harvard Education Press.

- Hitchcock, C. H., Meyer, A., & Rose, D. H. (2005). *The universally designed classroom: Accessible curriculum and digital technologies.* Cambridge, MA: Harvard Education Press.

- Rappolt-Schlichtmann, G., Daley, S. G., & Rose, L. T. (2012). *A research reader in universal design for learning.* Cambridge, MA: Harvard Education Press.

- Rose, D. H., & Meyer, A. (2002). *Teaching every student in the digital age: Universal design for learning.* Alexandria, VA: ASCD.

- Rose, D. H., and Meyer, A. (2006). *A practical reader in universal design for learning.* Cambridge, MA: Harvard Education Press.

# B

# Professional Learning Community Resources

Learning about UDL is a great opportunity for teams of teachers. Having like-minded individuals around you will make the transition to UDL simpler and more rewarding. If you have colleagues in your school who are interested, join together and earn some professional development points, as well. If there is no one at your school, connect to other practitioners virtually. I encourage you to connect on Twitter using #udlchat.

Also, remember that presentations for all chapters will be available on the website if you'd like to present them at your PLC meetings.

## PLC OBJECTIVES

As a result of the learning experiences throughout this text, participants will become more cognizant of the fundamental concepts of UDL. Participants will be able to perform each of the following:

- Differentiate between content and methods standards to reflect knowledge of UDL in PLC Assignment #1

- Create a choice assessment to guide students toward one standard in PLC Assignment #2

- Create an literacy trekker, an assignment that has multiple scaffolds for students of all ability levels in PLC Assignment #3

- Create an electronic handout that provides options for audio and visual learners in PLC Assignment #4

**TABLE B-1:** PLC Sample Outline

| SESSION | TOPIC | ACTIVITY OR ASSIGNMENT TO COMPLETE BEFORE NEXT MEETING |
|---|---|---|
| Before first meeting | | Read introduction and Chapter 1. |
| 1 | In the PLC, view presentations on introduction and Chapter 1. Also, discuss the questions at the end of Chapter 1. | Read Chapters 2–3. |
| 2 | View presentations on Chapters 2–3. Discuss the questions at the ends of chapters. | Read Chapters 4–5.<br><br>Design PLC Assignment #1 and use with students.<br><br>Design PLC Assignment #2 and use with students. |
| 3 | View presentations on Chapters 4–5. Discuss the questions at the ends of chapters. At end of meeting, present PLC Assignments #1–2 with student work exemplars. Be sure to reflect on students' reaction to UDL. | Read Chapters 6–7.<br><br>Design PLC Assignment #3 and use with students. |
| 4 | View presentations on Chapters 6–7. Discuss the questions at the ends of chapters. At end of meeting, share PLC Assignment #3 with student work exemplars. | Finish book.<br><br>PLC Assignment #4. |
| 5 | View presentations on Chapters 8–12. Answer all relevant discussion questions. Present PLC Assignment #4 to colleagues (make sure you have a projector available) and celebrate your UDL implementation. | |

# C

# PLC Assignment Rubric

|  | EXCEEDS STANDARDS | MEETS STANDARDS | NOT YET |
|---|---|---|---|
| Content | The product exceeds the objective of the assignment by carefully expressing content appropriate for task, purpose, and audience. | The product meets the objective of the assignment by expressing content that is appropriate for task, purpose, and audience. | The product is close to meeting the objectives of the assignment, but the purpose, or audience don't align well to the task. |
| Organization | Regardless of the format of the assignment, ideas are logically organized and developed; transitions easily connect content and ideas. | Regardless of the format of the assignment, ideas are logically organized and developed; there are some missing transitions, which may be confusing. | The product proceeds logically, but some transitions or organization problems impede flow |

|  | **EXCEEDS STANDARDS** | **MEETS STANDARDS** | **NOT YET** |
|---|---|---|---|
| UDL application | Practical application of UDL principles is established. Aspects from all three networks are present. | Some practical application of UDL principles is established. Aspects from at least two networks are present. | Very little practical application of UDL principles is established. Aspects from one network are present. |
| Language conventions | Grammar is consistently accurate; subjects agree with verbs; pronouns agree with antecedents; spelling and punctuation are accurate; and there are no typographical errors. | Grammar is accurate; noun/verb agreement, and pronoun/antecedent agreement is mostly accurate; few errors in spelling and punctuation; and there are no typographical errors. | Sentences are generally correct in structure; may display isolated serious errors or frequent minor errors that do not interfere with meaning or do not greatly distract the reader. |

# References

Anyon, J. (1980). Social class and the hidden curriculum of work. *Journal of Education, 162*(1), 67–92.

Beach, K.D., Sanchez, V., Flynn, L.J., & O'Connor, R.E. (2015). Teaching academic vocabulary to adolescents with learning disabilities. *Teaching Exceptional Children, 48*(1), 36–44.

Boyles, N. (2013). Closing in on close reading. *Educational Leadership, 70*(4), 36–41.

Brown, K.M., Anfara, V.A. Jr., & Roney, K. (2004). Student achievement in high-performing suburban middle schools and low-performing urban middle schools: Plausible explanations for the differences. *Education and Urban Society, 36*(4), 428–456.

Chall, J.S. (2000). *The academic achievement challenge: What really works in the classroom.* New York: Guilford Press.

Dulaney, S.K., Hallam, P.R., & Wall, G. (2013). Superintendent perceptions of multi-tiered systems of support (MTSS): Obstacles and opportunities for school system reform. *AASA Journal of Scholarship & Practice, 10*(2), 30–45.

DuFour, R. & Reeves, D. (2016). The futility of PLC lite. *Phi Delta Kappan, 97*(6), p.69–71.

Dweck, C.S. (2006). *Mindset: The new psychology of success.* New York: Random House.

Every Student Succeeds Act of 2015. Pub.L. 114–95.

Fenstermacher, G.D., & Richardson, V. (2005). On making determinations of quality teaching. *Teachers College Record, 107*(1), 186–213.

Ferguson, R.F. (2012). Can student surveys measure teaching quality? *Phi Delta Kappan, 94*(3), 24–28.

Frattura, E., & Capper, C. (2016). Integrated comprehensive systems for equity series. Retrieved from https://www.icsequity.org

Fuqua, J. (1985). Seven strategies for teaching context clues. *The Reading Teacher, 38*(6), 585–587.

Goddard, R.D., Hoy, W.K., & Hoy, A.W. (2000). Collective teacher efficacy: Its meaning, measure, and impact on student achievement. *American Educational Research Journal, 37*(2), 479–507.

Hall, T.E., Meyer, A., & Rose, D.H. (2012). *Universal design for learning in the classroom: Practical applications.* New York, NY: Guilford.

Hall, T., Strangman, N., & Meyer, A. (2003). *Differentiated instruction and implications for UDL implementation.* Wakefield, MA: National Center on Accessing the General Curriculum.

Hobson, C.J., Strupeck, D., Griffin, A., Szostek, J., & Rominger, A.S. (2014). Teaching MBA students teamwork and team leadership skills: An empirical evaluation of a classroom educational program. *American Journal of Business Education, 7*(3), 191–212.

Indrisano, R., & Chall, J.S. (1995). Literacy development. *Journal of Education, 177*(1), 63–83.

Literacy Design Collaborative. (2013). LDC template task collection 2.0. Retrieved from https://ldc.org/

McEwan, E.K. (2007). *40 ways to support struggling readers in content classrooms: Grades 6–12.* Thousands Oaks, CA: Corwin Press.

McKee-Waddell, S. (2015). Digital literacy: Bridging the gap with digital writing tools. *Delta Kappa Gamma Bulletin, 82*(1), 26–31.

Merton, R. (1948). The self-fulfilling prophecy. *Antioch Review, 8*(2), 193–210.

Meyer, A., Rose, D.H., & Gordon, D. (2014). *Universal design for learning: Theory and practice.* Wakefield, MA: CAST Professional Publishing. Also published online at http://udltheorypractice.cast.org.

Moir, E. (1990). Phases of first-year teaching. *California New Teacher Project Newsletter.* Sacramento, CA: California Department of Education. Online at www.newteachercenter.org/blog/phases-first-year-teaching.

Pink, Daniel H. (2009). *Drive: The Surprising Truth about What Motivates Us.* New York: Riverhead.

Prime, G.M., & Miranda, R.J. (2006). "Urban public high school teachers' beliefs about science learner characteristics: Implications for curriculum. *Urban Education, 41*(5), 506–532.

Prior, L.A., Willson, A., & Martinez, M. (2012). Picture this; Visual literacy as a pathway to character understanding. *The Reading Teacher 66*(3), 195–206.

Puntambekar, S., & Hübscher, R. (2005). Tools for scaffolding students in a complex learning environment: What have we gained and what have we missed? *Educational Psychologist, 40*(1), 1–12.

Routman, R. (2003). *Reading essentials: The specifics you need to teach reading well.* Portsmouth, NH: Heinemann.

Sinek, S. (2011). *Start with why: How great leaders inspire everyone to take action.* New York, NY: Portfolio/Penguin.

Trilling, B. & Fadel, C. (2009). *21st century skills: Learning for life in our times.* San Francisco, CA: Jossey-Bass.

Vygotsky, L. (1978). Mind in society: The development of higher psychological processes. Cambridge, *MA: Harvard University Press.*

Yang, L. (2009). Scaffolding the unbelievable: Understanding light and vision. *Journal of College Science Teaching, 38*(6), 54–57.

Waldron, N. & McLeskey, J. (2001). Helping schools include all learners. *Intervention in School and Clinic 36*(3), 175–81.

# About the Author

**Katie Novak, Ed.D.**, is assistant superintendent of the Groton-Dunstable Regional School District in Massachusetts.

With more than a decade of both classroom and college teaching experience, Novak continues to teach and present workshops nationally and internationally focusing on teacher implementation of UDL. Following are some professional highlights:

- Earned a doctorate from Boston University in curriculum and teaching in English/language arts and literacy, K–12. Dr. Novak also completed graduate studies in both language acquisition and reading instruction.

- Holds both a teaching and an administrator's license.

- She is the co-author of two other books: *UDL in the Cloud! How to Design and Deliver Online Education Using Universal Design for Learning*, and *Universally Designed Leadership: Applying UDL to Districts and Schools*, both published by CAST Professional Publishing.

- Independent presenter for CAST and a member of CAST's UDL Professional Learning Cadre. Invited to present at numerous workshops, including Harvard University's summer session focused on designing and implementing a UDL curriculum.

- Selected by the Bill & Melinda Gates Foundation to attend and present at the prestigious ECET2 (Elevating and Celebrating Excellence in Teachers and Teaching) conference and the National Teacher Voice Convening, both of which celebrate the work of teacher leaders in the country.

- Selected by the Teaching Channel to be featured in a series of videos about teacher excellence.

- Teaches graduate-level courses focused on UDL implementation to PK-12 teachers and higher education faculty.

She'd love to hear from you! Visit www.katienovakudl.com, e-mail novak414@gmail.com, or connect to @KatieNovakUDL on Twitter.

# Acknowledgments

For this second edition, I'd like to thank three teachers who made a huge difference in my life. All of them inspired me to work hard, love the process of learning, and seek out a framework that would allow me engage and inspire learners, like they did for me. My only hope is to continue to share the UDL message so future teachers can follow in their footsteps.

Mrs. Kraus, I will never forget how you pulled me aside after class and told me that I was sitting on wasted potential. Before you, I didn't see the value of becoming an expert learner. You lit a fire under me and changed the trajectory of my education. For that I am forever grateful.

Coach Seal, even though you had me run the 4x400 on a fractured leg, I will never forget how hard you pushed me to succeed. Whether it was early morning pancake runs, never ending box jumps, or hours of interval sprints, you taught me that if I wanted something, I had to fight for it. When things in life get challenging, I can hear your voice screaming at me from the finish line.

Clark Knowles, you taught me the craft of writing, the creative process, and the power of revision, revision, and more revision. Your class was my favorite at UNH. You were the master of designing a motivating, collaborative classroom sanctuary that we never wanted to leave. After spending a semester with you, I knew without a doubt that I wanted to be a writer.

# Index

**Note**: Italicized page numbers indicate figures; underlined page numbers indicate Web links.

## P

paragraphs, writing, 160–161, 165

PBWorks, using to enhance digital writing, 94

Penflip, using to enhance digital writing, 94

"pep rally," having night before taking tests, 199–200

perception, providing options for, 19, 21, 25, 70–73

performance. *See* student performance

persistence. *See* effort and persistence

phases of UDL implementation, 8

physical action, providing options for, 19, 21, 27–28, 79

physical education standards
Elementary, 102
Secondary, 103

picture clues, response to, 174–175

*Picture This: Visual Literacy as a Pathway to Character Understanding*, 153–154

Pink, Daniel H., 32, 219

pizza dough, 183–184

PLC (professional learning community)
assignment rubric, 215–216
core questions, 9
effectiveness, 9

forming, 8
joining, 1, 10
meaningfulness of, 9
objectives, 213–214
sample outline, 214

PLC assignments
content standards, 128–129
electronic handout, 206
examining standards, 104–105
scaffolded reading, 158

poetry, writing, 118

posters, creating, 118–119

posting standards, 100

PowerPoint presentations, 204

Powtoon presentation software, 118, 205

Pre-K students, introducing UDL to, 55

Prepare and Phase 1, 8

presentational barriers, 24

presentations, free applications, 204–205

Prezi presentations, 119, 204–205

Prime & Medina, student failure, 14

Prior, Willson, and Martinez, 154, 219

problem and solution, role in text structure, 148

processes, evaluating complexity of, 76

# S

scaffolded instruction
active engagement, 142
designing, 108-109
intersubjectivity, 142
ongoing diagnosis, 142
overview, 141-144
theory of, 107
transfer of responsibility, 142
scaffolded reading. *See also* vocabulary
activating prior knowledge, 150
analyzing opinions and arguments, 151
asking questions, 151
close reading, 153
comprehensive literacy instruction, 144-145
critical thinking skills, 151
expository text structure, 148-149
literacy trekker, 154-157
making inferences, 150
monitoring and clarifying, 151
paraphrasing, 152
reading strategies, 149-154
searching the text, 151
summarizing, 152
text structures, 146-147
visual literacy, 153-154
visualizing, 152

scaffolded writing, 177-178. *See also* writing business letter and business e-mail
assignment organization, 160-162
body paragraphs, 161, 165
brainstorming, 159
compound sentences, 165
conclusion paragraph, 161, 165
content and development, 165-166
drafting, 159-160
focus and organization, 165-166
foreshadowing, 163
grammar, usage, and mechanics, 165
hooks, 160, 165
information from text, 163
introduction paragraph, 160-161, 163, 165
language conventions, 163
main idea, 165
organization, 163
overview, 158-159
publishing, 167-168
revising and editing, 164-167
revision process, 167
rubric for explorer letter, 163-164
sensory details, 165
sentences, 165-166

work exemplars, providing, 75–76

WPM (words per minute) rates, building for keyboarding skills, 207

writing business letter and business e-mail, 121–122. See *also* scaffolded writing

writing lesson, designing, 17

writing prompts, adding details to, 166

writing tools, 93–94

written responses, barriers to, 26

## Y

Yang, Li-hsuan, 110, 219

## Z

Zentangle doodling activity, 60

ZPD (zone of proximal development), 107